SECRET LETTERS
FROM
THE RAILWAY

SECRET LETTERS FROM THE RAILWAY

The Remarkable Record of Charles Steel, a Japanese POW

by

BRIAN BEST

Pen & Sword
MILITARY

First published in Great Britain in 2004 by
Pen & Sword Military
an imprint of
Pen & Sword Books Ltd
47 Church Street
Barnsley
South Yorkshire
S70 2AS

ISBN 1 84415 118 2

A CIP catalogue record for this book is
available from the British Library

Typeset in 11/13 Sabon by
Phoenix Typesetting, Auldgirth, Dumfriesshire

Printed and bound in England by
CPI UK

For a complete list of Pen & Sword titles please contact
PEN & SWORD BOOKS LIMITED
47 Church Street, Barnsley, South Yorkshire, S70 2AS, England
E-mail: enquiries@pen-and-sword.co.uk
Website: www.pen-and-sword.co.uk

Prisoner in the Bag
by Robert Hope

Captured, taken prisoner and in the bag
Sounds so strange yet means the same
To be transported from the fray
The enemy to guard through night and day
Incarcerated behind barbed wire fences
Little to do, except time to while away
Long endless days and cold, cold nights
Now imprisoned and unable to fight
Many a long year through endless humdrum
But we were lucky with this weary boredom

Of our comrades out in the East
Sent to fight and the enemy to beat
Outmanoeuvred and taken out
Too far away, they would have to do without
The enemy to take and be beaten down
With fist or boot and rifle butt
Starved, abused and worked to death
Lose zest for life and to die within
If not disease, work and beatings, the bayonet will
Bring to an end so soft a kill

But such is war fate served an unjust hand
Who ever said war was grand
A soldier death in battle to die
But what of those who died a prisoner
Who served and suffered right to the end
Yet all were unable to self defend
Less we forget, but always remember
The nightmares and cries of the survivor
Through the harshness all suffered pain
And those that died, did not die in vain

Acknowledgments

When I was asked if I was interested in editing the letters kept by a prisoner of the Japanese, my initial reaction was that the subject matter would be both grim and depressing. I am glad I did not turn down the project, for I found in the letters of Charles Steel one of the most uplifting reading experiences I have ever enjoyed.

For this, I am grateful to Margaret and David Sargent for putting their trust in me and allowing full access to all of Charles and Louise Steel's papers.

I must also thank the staffs at the Imperial War Museum Library and Crowborough and Tunbridge Wells Libraries for their help and suggestions.

Contents

Introduction

Charles Steel had a most unfortunate war. He was one of the unlucky few who participated in two of the greatest disasters to befall the British Army – Dunkirk and the fall of Singapore. He not only survived both experiences but emerged mentally stronger and surprisingly unembittered. His story is well worth the telling, for he was a survivor of that most appalling experience that could befall a soldier captured during the Pacific War – he was held a prisoner of war by the Japanese.

For four long years he and his fellow prisoners endured cruelties and hardships that are, today, almost beyond comprehension. Many men did not survive the harrowing experiences of starvation, disease, slave labour and the barbaric acts of their captors. Unable to cope with the nightmare into which they had been pitched, so many suffered mentally and just gave up as if preferring death to any faint hope of eventual salvation.

Steel was not one of these *Muselmanner*, the German slang for the 'walking dead', whose divine spark had been extinguished within. Instead, he refused to be paralysed by a denial of what was happening to him and set about adopting a goal he could focus upon. Something that would kindle a fighting spirit so he would be able to trudge through the darkness toward a far distant pinprick of light.

Within days of being captured at Singapore, Charles wrote his first letter to Louise, his wife of just ninety days. From the chaos of that debacle, when he felt sure they would be shortly repatriated, Charles began writing letters that were never sent. Even when he was at his lowest ebb, a sick, starved slave on the Burma-Siam railway, he kept writing to his beloved Louise, relating not only the everyday horrors but also his observations of his captors, his fellow POWs, the surrounding countryside and wildlife. Above all, the letters were declarations of love written by a man who focused on his young wife as his personal reason to rise above the surrounding hopelessness and will himself to survive. Risking punishment – for the Japanese forbade any writing or sketching that would record their inhuman behaviour – Charles managed to document life as a slave labourer on one of the most remarkable engineering feats of the twentieth century. The letters were a form of record, but written for Louise's eyes – only and with no thought that they would be read by a curious posterity.

Steel wrote and hid 183 letters during captivity and another thirty-two after the Japanese surrender. They show a man who retained his sanity, humanity and even a sense of humour under the most testing of circumstances. Far from being a broken man, he put his experiences behind him and made his dreams during captivity come true.

Chapter 1

The Early Years

My Dear Wife
I am a Prisoner of War.

These stark opening words written from Changi, just after the
fall of Singapore, were the first of nearly 200 letters written, but
never sent, by Battery Sergeant Major Charles Steel. They were
written when there seemed hope that he and his fellow captives
might be exchanged and repatriated. This was the time of
phoney captivity, when the Japanese left the British and
Australians to their own devices and the only suffering was poor
food, overcrowding and boredom. When Steel wrote that he was
a prisoner of the Japanese, it did not have the fearful connota-
tion it was soon to gain. Indeed, those British officers who were
familiar with the Japanese Army during the 1920s and 1930s
did not predict the dramatic change of behaviour towards their
prisoners. It was pointed out that, during the war of 1904–05,
the Japanese treated their Russian prisoners in an exemplary
fashion.

In the meantime, Charles had plenty of time to recollect on the
unkind fates that had directed him to his present predicament.

Charles Wilfred Steel was born on 7 December 1916 in a
middle-class area of Bow in London's East End. His father was
a manager, who later rose to become a partner with the
brokerage firm Mardorf, Peach in the Corn Exchange. The

railway ran through a cutting below the bottom of his parent's garden and one of Charles's earliest recollections was of the steam trains that journeyed to and from Liverpool Street Station. This early fascination for steam engines remained with him for all his life.

Tragedy struck when his mother was one of the many thousands who succumbed to the flu pandemic of 1918 and it was left to her two spinster sisters to care for him. His father married his secretary and Charles's new stepmother proved to be a loving substitute and soon provided Charles with a younger brother named Ken.

Charles was an academically bright child and in 1928 gained a scholarship to the Sir George Moneaux Grammar School in Walthamstow. Both the school and his father encouraged outdoor pursuits and physical fitness, something for which Charles would later be thankful. When he was just seventeen, he left school having matriculated with seven subjects. He had a good head for figures and, with his father's help, joined a firm of stockbrokers. It was a career in which he remained all his working life.

Once he had left school, the family moved from the East End to the comparatively rural area of Shirley, on the Kent/Surrey border, not far from Bromley. Charles immediately took to the whole ambience of working in the City and relished the opportunity of trading on the dealing floor at the Stock Exchange. One of the social activities available to City workers and, indeed was encouraged, was the joining of a Territorial Army regiment.

The most prestigious City regiment was the Honorable Artillery Company at Finsbury Square but, in 1937, Charles chose to join the 97 (Kent Yeomanry) Field Regiment Royal Artillery, 387th Battery, Queen's Own West Kent Yeomanry, for it was based at Bromley Common, close to his home. Within a short time Gunner Steel had made a whole new circle of friends and took on new pursuits. One of the activities he enjoyed was to cycle around the lovely Kent countryside. In those pre-war days there was very little traffic and cycling clubs filled the roads most weekends. It was during one of these club outings that

Charles noticed and was instantly attracted to a slim young lady who was happy to encourage his advances. Her name was Louise Crane and she lived at the nearby village of North Cray. They soon found they had many interests in common, including the part-time army. To Charles's mild irritation, he found that his new girlfriend was a sergeant in the ATS and, throughout their respective service careers, she continued to outrank him.

The years between the wars were difficult for the Territorial Army. Lack of training grants and equipment, few experienced instructors and a general public apathy made the Territorials little more than a social club. The gathering war clouds and the passing of the Conscription Act of 1938 changed this with a large influx of volunteers. Unfortunately, the shortage of officers and experienced NCO's seriously hampered training and organization. This was uncomfortably brought home during the annual TA camp and manoeuvres at Okehampton in the spring of 1939.

The previous summer, Charles had enjoyed a rather jolly time at his first camp on the South Downs near Seaford. In glorious summer weather, the young volunteers were put through gun drill, but there had been no firing of their vintage 18-pounder guns. Instead, there had been plenty of polishing until the old artillery pieces gleamed in the bright sunshine. At the end of the fortnight, everyone agreed that it had been very healthy and pleasant. The camp at Okehampton on Dartmoor was to prove very different.

A combination of misplaced enthusiasm, the expectation of war against Germany and a breakdown in communication found over 2,000 volunteers pitching tents in an area designed for about 1,000. Torrential driving rain soon turned the camp into a morass and many tents were washed away. The hospital, which had only three beds, could not cope with the steady stream of sick, and the cooking facilities were similarly limited. Men were reduced to sleeping in nearby barns and stables, while those who drove down in their own cars spent several uncomfortable sleepless nights in their vehicles. This shambles caused such an uproar that Lionel Hore-Belisha, the Secretary of State for War, was given a torrid time in the House of Commons. He laid the blame on the commanding officers for sending duplicate units of reservists and volunteers to attend with their original units.

Once the rains relented, Charles and his colleagues were able to be trained in the use of more modern ordnance like the 25-pounder and the 4.5-inch howitzer and to experience the firing of live rounds. This was just as well, for the Kent Yeomanry was about be thrown in at the deep end.

Chapter 2

The Fall of France

On 1 September, the day the Germans began their invasion of Poland, Charles Steel and his comrades responded to the Reserve and Volunteers Calling Out Notice and reported the following day to the Bromley Common HQ. Unlike the regular army, the TA had no mobilization stores at their depots, so all equipment had to be collected or commandeered from around the south-east. In the ensuing confusion and clamour, it was no surprise that mistakes were made. The day before the 97th entrained at Maidstone, it was discovered that the Ordnance had issued over 700 sets of webbing equipment without belts. Some of the lorries that had been commandeered had to be hastily painted to prevent advertising 'Kent's Best Beer' and the merits of a couple of rival laundries to the natives of northern France.

There was barely enough time for Charles to say his goodbyes to Louise before he left for Southampton and, on 23 September, set sail on the SS *Bruges* for Cherbourg. The 97th was on its way to join the British Expeditionary Force in France and was the first TA regiment to arrive. By stages, over the following weeks, the regiment travelled through Normandy until they finally dug in at Moncheaux, on the Somme. The new commanding officer, Lieutenant Colonel Franklin Lushington, recognized that his command was not trained to the same pitch as their regular army counterparts, so he organized for the regiment to visit and train at the ranges at Sissons and Marieux. Despite their comparative lack of expertise, Lushington felt that the Territorials had two great advantages over the Regulars. The standard of education amongst all ranks was generally higher and they all came from the same area, giving them a greater bonding.

This was the time of the 'Phoney War' when the enemy were invisible and almost wholly non-belligerent. Much time was spent digging defences which, in the event, were never occupied. On 5 December, they were paid a visit by King George and later by the Duke of Gloucester. During this lull before the storm, apart from the bitter cold, life was reasonably pleasant and the new colonel tried to keep spirits from flagging. A Christmas party was thrown in the local village hall and everyone down to the most junior gunner drank champagne. This was followed by a memorable New Year's lunch at Bapaume, which was rounded off by a pitched snowball fight. This all helped to foster a real *esprit de corps* and morale was high. There was plenty of time for short leaves and the nearest source of recreation was the town of Albert, still showing scars from the Battle of the Somme. The immediate threat of war appeared to recede and Charles was able to take a ten-day leave in February. Predictably, he spent most of his leave visiting Louise, whose unit was stationed at Brighton. With a mixture of pride and irritation, he learned that she had just been promoted and referred to her as 'my own particular sergeant major'. Like many couples at that time of high uncertainty, they decided to get married.

Soon after Charles rejoined his regiment, they were sent to Perenchies near Lille. Here the regiment suffered their first casualties when a First World War shell exploded under the cook's fire and injured three men. In April, the Germans began their long-anticipated advance into Belgium and France; the 'Phoney War' was over. The 97th was incorporated into the 5th Division and ordered into Belgium to help counter the German invasion. They reached Ghoy, south of Brussels and so began weeks of confusion, with orders that were countermanded almost as soon as they were issued. Before they had time to dig in, the 97th was ordered to retreat to Escourt, where the 5th Division was told to hold the Brussels-Charleroi Canal. With the French on their right falling back and the Belgians collapsing on their left, the 5th Division was again ordered to immediately retire to Seclin in order to 'straighten the line'.

During this manoeuvre, Charles saw the effects of war for the first time. The roads were packed with refugees, carrying all that they could manage in trucks, cars, horse-drawn carts, bikes, prams or on their bent backs. When night fell, the 97th was not allowed to use its headlights and sleep was impossible. They crawled through Tournai, which was in flames and they felt very vulnerable from an attack by the Luftwaffe.

Finally they reached Seclin, only to be sent on to the mining village of Estevilles. Due to the refugee-congested road, it took the exhausted yeomen a further seven hours to cover just ten miles. Here they took over the French gun positions and found the village deserted except for cows and pigs that roamed aimlessly about. It was here that Charles's battery fired its first shots in anger in a brief exchange with the Germans, before being ordered to pull back once more; another night retreat through a landscape littered with the detritus of war and panic. The worst part of this constant relocating was not knowing what was going on with the rest of the front. They did not know that the French had caved in at Sedan and that they were in full retreat to the south. The Germans were swiftly advancing west and outflanking the Allies in Belgium. The collapse and surrender of the Belgians exposed the British left flank in the north. Confusion and alarm gripped the Allies, as the Germans appeared to be everywhere, even in the rear. The Panzer divisions had outstripped their infantry and punched holes in the Allies' lines. If the Allied commanders had but known that the German armour was overextended and the German commander was on the point of ordering a halt, a concerted stand and attack may have changed the course of the battle. Instead, an irreversible momentum had been set in motion, which would not stop until Dunkirk was reached.

The Germans were close on the heels of the Allies as they fell back and, after another skirmish, they were ordered to fall back on Verlingham. Starting at dusk, the 97th retreated through burning and deserted villages and the roads and fields were littered with the debris of a routed population. At Verlingham, they found that the inhabitants who had cheered them on their way just a few days before, were now sullen and resigned to join the swelling tide of refugees. One point in favour of occupying deserted villages was that the ration-starved soldiers could rely on finding plenty to eat and drink.

During this confused and frightening time, the Germans had mastery of the skies. The choked roads made easy targets, which the Luftwaffe was not slow to exploit. During a typically slow march, a plane swooped low over a gridlocked area and every available gun opened fire for a couple of miles radius, including those of the 97th. Such concentrated fire succeeded in downing the plane, which crashed into Plugstreet Wood, another famous name from the First World War. To everyone's dismay, the wreckage was found to be that of a RAF plane and the two British crew were dead. It was the first British plane Charles had seen since the Germans began their invasion.

On 28 May, there began the retreat towards the last Channel port left in Allied hands; Dunkirk. Charles and his comrades joined a vast throng of lorries, guns, soldiers and civilians that were slowly moving down the poplar-lined roads towards the sea. It was truly a demoralized and apprehensive rabble that was seeking refuge in the last Allied held enclave. The already fraught emotions were exacerbated by the contempt the British had for the French for capitulating so easily and the distrust
the French felt for the British, who were making haste to cross the Channel. Charles saw this breakdown in Allied relationships brutally illustrated. Colonel Lushington graphically recollected that it was the last and worst night of the retreat.

All semblance of order and discipline seemed to have dis-
appeared. There was no panic but the men were just too tired
to care and lorries and cars double-banked and crawled and
halted and moved on again, then halted once more whilst their

tired drivers fell asleep at their wheels. Units were mixed up in inextricable confusion and to make matters worse large numbers of French soldiers on horseback and on foot kept crowding in among us and pushing their way past, making anything like continuous movement impossible. At one point, a lorry had fallen sideways into a large bomb crater in the middle of the road thereby completely blocking it. (Major) David Warner had collected a party of men and was trying to lift it back on to its wheels. The panic-stricken French soldiers, however, refused to stop and, in their eagerness to get on, kept pushing the working party to one side. At last, exasperated, Warner drew his revolver and in his best French threatened to shoot the next man who failed to stop when ordered. His French, however, was evidently not good enough, or perhaps they were too frightened to listen, for it was not until he shot one that the lorry was eventually lifted, the crater filled up and the road cleared.

The 97th was now passing through the old Ypres battlefield, which still bore scars after twenty-five years. They slowly passed through Poperinghe as it was being shelled but, mercifully, the Luftwaffe did not appear and take advantage of their helpless position. Here the 5th Division held the line of the Ypres-Comines canal and repulsed a concerted German assault. A heavy downpour of rain in late afternoon dampened the fierceness of the attacks, and the exhausted men were able to continue their retreat along the narrow Flanders roads.

When the 97th crossed the Yser River at Eikhoek, they received orders to destroy all their equipment. Driving into a field, Charles and his comrades set about their vehicles with axes and sledgehammers. The gun barrels were wrecked with guncotton and their breechblocks buried. The 97th was now truly a regiment without a purpose. The footsore and hungry men then turned to cover the final twelve miles to the coast at De Panne. From there they were directed south, crossing into France until they collapsed, exhausted on the dunes at Bray. Here they spent a miserable night huddled together in their greatcoats. In the morning they were ordered to march back to De Penne, which was in total chaos. Colonel Lushington learned that boats were waiting at Bray and that they should immediately return to the dunes. Unable to face yet another march, the 97th got hold of whatever vehicles were to be had and the regiment headed back down the coast in a motley convoy of a large bus, bikes and horses. When they reached Bray, there was no sign of any of the promised boats. The beach-master ordered the Territorials to return again to De Panne but Lushington decided to go on to Dunkirk to the south. The sight that greeted them was one of organized chaos. Thousands of men were lined up along the promenade and the beaches were crowded with soldiers trudging slowly towards the quays about two miles to the south. Huge fires were burning out of control around the dock area, while out to sea was a flotilla of assorted vessels ranging from naval destroyers to tugs and ferryboats. Small craft were inshore, picking up men who waded into the shallows and delivering them to the parent ships. In the confusion, the yeoman became separated from each other. Lushington and a group of about forty waded out and were picked up by a boat that put them on board HMS *Winchelsea*.

Charles and most of his companions had joined the throng making their way to the East Mole, a rather flimsy wooden structure, which was only eight feet wide and jutted 1,400 yards out into the harbour. These were anxious and dangerous hours, for the Germans were constantly bombing and firing on the crowded beaches and the rescue ships. The skies above were filled with the diminuendo and crescendo sounds of diving and weaving aircraft as the RAF sought to shield the helpless masses below from the Luftwaffe. After the heavy criticism the RAF received for their poor showing during the Battle for France, they answered their detractors with a better performance at Dunkirk. At the beginning of the evacuation, their frequent and outnumbered patrols had little effect in protecting the helpless soldiers, who reviled the invisible 'Brylcream Boys'. Quickly learning from this, Fighter Command flew fewer sorties but in greater strength. This change of tactics produced a dramatic change of fortune for, on 30 May, RAF fighters downed seventy-six enemy for the loss of just five of their own. Black smoke from the fuel depot on the west side of the harbour darkened the sky and filled the nostrils. These fires sent a dense black plume over the port which did much to conceal the harbour from the Luftwaffe. The distant sounds of gunfire could be heard from inland as the unlucky and doomed members of the rearguard held back the German army until their comrades could be evacuated.

Like a huge football crowd, the silent soldiers shuffled slowly forward to the bottleneck of the narrow mole. Several vessels at a time were alongside and being steadily filled with men. Naval and army harbour masters were managing to keep good order as overfull ships pulled off to make way for the next vessel, which had to negotiate a passage between the wrecks visible above the waves. Charles spent the whole of 31 May patiently queuing until finally he was able to board the last destroyer that evening. He wrote;

> HMS Express *was on her seventh and last trip to Dunkirk. She made a magnificent sight as, with her guns blazing and German aircraft attacking her, she backed against the broken mole to allow us to jump aboard. On our way back across, she was engaged by coastal guns and further waves of aircraft.*

HMS *Express* left Dunkirk at 4 p.m., evacuating the naval pier party and 611 troops. Two months later, *Express* and two other destroyers sailed into a German minefield off Texel. *Express* had her bows blown off, but managed to be towed back to England. After repairs, she served with the Canadian navy as RCN *Gatineau*.

It was not until much later that Charles and his comrades realized just how remarkable was their escape. Out of a British Expeditionary Force total of 350,000, approximately 30,000 had been killed, wounded, were missing or made prisoner. The bulk of the British army had been saved and it was this aspect that was emphasized and not the fact they had all but been overwhelmed by a superior enemy and forced to leave nearly all their arms and equipment behind.

All the evacuees who were landed at Dover had time for a meal and a short rest before they were sent by train to camps, mostly away from southern England. For Charles, his destination was Lichfield in Staffordshire. As the dust settled and the mixed-up units were sorted out, Charles was sent to Okehampton, the scene of the infamous flooded camp of 1939, where the remnants of his unit were concentrated. In June, Charles was granted leave to be reunited with the family and Louise.

Chapter 3

Changes

Instead of returning to Okehampton, Charles was ordered to Abergele in Wales. During July, he was detailed to travel to a Leeds company called Cement Ltd. Here, he and his colleagues collected a small column of emergency mobile pill-boxes called 'The Bison'. This heavy concrete structure, mounted on a chassis, was then driven from Leeds to Pembroke on a journey that Charles dryly described as 'an exciting experience'.

The period in Wales was spent mounting and manning naval guns on the docks at Swansea and along the neighbouring coast. Quite suddenly, Charles received a transfer out of the 97th and into the 336 Field Battery, 135 (North Herts Yeomanry) Field Regiment. With this transfer came an overdue promotion to Troop Sergeant. Any approach to parity of rank with his fiancée was short-lived, however, for Louise shortly gained her commission in the ATS.

135th were at that time stationed in Norfolk, were an inexperienced regiment and, in the words of one of its officers, . . . *'more distinguished socially than militarily'*. There was a generous sprinkling of minor titled landowners, professionals and academics and the mess was filled with dialogue and accents that would have inspired P.G.Wodehouse.

For the next year the 135th were stationed at places as far apart as Lockerbie and Plymouth. This seemingly easy time was interrupted with fire-watching duty in Liverpool during the blitz, when Charles wrote this piece of doggerel;

If you can keep yourself from going crackers
At all the things that you're advised to do
When Hitler sends his horrid Air Attackers
With squibs and bombs to try to frighten you,
If you can hear that hellish banshee warning
Without that sinking feeling in your breast,
If you can sleep in dug-outs till the morning
And never feel you ought to have more rest,
If you can laugh at every black-out stumble,
Nor murmur when you cannot find a pub,
If you can eat your rations and not grumble
About the wicked price you pay for grub,
If you can keep depression down to zero
And view it all as just a bit of fun,
Then, Sir, you'll be a bloody hero,
And what is more, you'll be the only one.

Granted compassionate leave, Charles and Louise were married on 18 January 1941 at St James's Church, North Cray. A few days' honeymoon at Llandudno was all they could grab before they both had to return to their units.

During the next six months, Charles took part in half a dozen training courses and according to the reports, he was regarded as *'quick, alert, intelligent and takes command'*. The carrot of a commission was dangled and Charles began to see life through the eyes of an officer. Alas, fate interrupted his undoubted step from non-commissioned to commissioned officer and it was to remain a bone of contention with him for the rest of his life.

In June, the 135th were stationed at Alderley Edge, described as England's wealthiest village. It was here that the command of the regiment passed to one of the war's most remarkable soldiers. Lieutenant Colonel Philip Toosey had served as a major in the 359 (West Lancashire) Medium Regiment during the Fall of France and its experiences had mirrored those of the 97th.

Toosey was a TA officer with ten years' experience and had trained his battery to the point where they had won the coveted King's Cup; a competition to find the best artillery battery in both the regular and territorial army.

When he took command of the 135th, he found an enthusiastic but largely untrained unit. This became all too apparent the first time they attended an artillery range in North Wales and managed to land shots on two villages outside the range. Weeding out a few of the more amateur-minded amongst his officers, Toosey's quiet leadership caused the regiment to undergo a great change. He organized an extensive period of training, which rapidly improved the regiment's gunnery skills and instilled a more professional attitude from his officers.

The 135th was part of the 18th Division, which was ordered to prepare for overseas duty. The general consensus was that it was destined for the Middle East, as the equipment had been ordered to be painted a sandy colour. There was a brief embarkation leave to spend with his new wife before Charles travelled to Greenock and boarded the MV *Sobieski*, which set sail on 28 October 1941.

The *Sobieski* was a small liner belonging to the Gdynia-America Line. With a limited number of cabins, most of the men had to get used to sleeping in hammocks in the confined spaces below decks. The Polish ship was one of eight ships making the perilous voyage across the North Atlantic and they were escorted by two destroyers and a flak ship. Halfway across, their Royal Navy escort was exchanged for an American one. In any event, the crossing was uneventful and the convoy made landfall at Halifax, Nova Scotia, on 9 November.

The following day, the 135th were trans-shipped to the larger and better appointed American liner *Washington* now renamed *Mount Vernon*. They were joined by the rest of the 18th Division, who were spread amongst three vessels, the other two being the *Wakefield* and the *West Point,* all former liners of the US Line.

Joined by three smaller troopships and accompanied by a huge US escort of an aircraft carrier, two heavy cruisers and eight destroyers, they left Halifax on 12 November and steamed south to the Caribbean as far as Trinidad, where they refuelled overnight. This massive support from the 'neutral' Americans came as a result of the meeting between Churchill and Roosevelt on board the *Prince of Wales* off Newfoundland in August, when the President acceded to Britain's request for help in shipping troops to the Middle East. Setting course south-east across the South Atlantic, the troops endured a long meandering trip. To fight off the tedium and frustration felt by all, Colonel Toosey organized special courses and physical exercises to keep his men up to the mark. The accommodation below decks was cramped, crowded, hot and smelly, so anything to get away from this foetid atmosphere was enthusiastically welcomed.

Cape Town was reached on 9 December and everyone enjoyed a welcome two-day leave in a city untouched by war. Just before they docked, the American crew informed their British guests that Japan had attacked the US Naval Base at Pearl Harbor and that they were now officially allies. The other sobering news came from south east Asia, where Japan had invaded Malaya and had sunk the pride of the Royal Navy, HMS *Prince of Wales* and the *Repulse*.

Parting from their American escort, the convoy left on 14 December and headed up the east coast of Africa to Mombasa, accompanied by the cruiser, HMS *Dorsetshire*.

Another few days were spent sampling the sleepy delights of Mombasa before they set sail once more. Charles and his companions still believed they were bound for Basra on the Persian Gulf but, within a short-time, the vessels were halted and a message came from *Dorsetshire* for the *Mount Vernon* to immediately change course and sail for Singapore via the Maldives. The other two vessels were ordered to Bombay, taking with them the regiment's guns and new 'quad' towing vehicles. *Mount Vernon* was chosen because of her greater speed, which stood a better chance against the enemy submarines that were known to be in Malayan waters, and also because she was carrying a complete brigade. She was joined by four merchant ships and escorted by HMS *Exeter* and *Ajax* of River Plate fame.

Chapter 4

Another Military Defeat

The first two years of the war found Britain and her allies un-prepared for the double assault from Germany and Japan. Like an under-prepared and ageing heavyweight boxer, she found herself pinned against the ropes and subjected to two devas-tating combination punches that all but felled her. First was the right-hook of the German blitzkrieg, which resulted in the Fall of France. Before she could recover, Japan delivered a crippling uppercut with the overrunning of Malaya and the Singapore capitulation.

The Fall of France and the Netherlands and the seemingly imminent collapse of Britain during the summer of 1940 emboldened Japan enough to advance into the Europeans' colonies in south-east Asia. Under the anti-colonist banner of a 'Greater East Asia Co-Prosperity Sphere', a new order under an enlightened and industrialized Japan would lead her backward neighbours to prosperity without the shackles of their European masters. The reality was brutally different, with a regime that was far more racist, vicious and exploitative than anything that white colonializm had ever inflicted.

The news from Singapore was bad. The Japanese Army had pushed rapidly down the Malay peninsular and were threaten-ing Singapore itself. Indeed, when the *Mount Vernon* approached, it was during a lull from the incessant air raids that had become a daily feature. Heavy black storm clouds obscured the island from the Japanese bombers, so the *Mount Vernon* and the rest of the convoy managed to dock unscathed at the Naval Dock Yard. On 13 January 1942, after nearly three months at sea, Charles and his comrades disembarked to the welcome of a drenching tropical storm. A miserable night was spent at their appointed camp at Nee Soon, while Colonel Toosey received instructions as to their role. The 135th was an artillery unit without guns or towing vehicles, for these were following with the rest of the 18th Division via Bombay. Toosey showed his stubborn nature when he refused to accept the Ordnance Department's dilatoriness in their handling of his request for 25-pounders. Persistent and hectoring visits wore down the resolve of the khaki 'jobsworths', and Toosey managed to obtain the regiment's full quota of guns. Towing vehicles, however, were in short supply, so they had to use whatever was available, including municipal dustcarts.

At this juncture, the mixed British/Indian/Australian army was trying to stem the Japanese advance into the southern Malay province of Johore; the final bulwark between Singapore island and the enemy. The whole Malayan debacle had been a catalogue of poor leadership and confusion. Barely trained Australian recruits were rushed up country and thrown into the front line. Similarly inexperienced Indian forces were no match for the crack Japanese regiments. Ill-sited airfields for non-existent aircraft and a lack of naval craft left the badly trained army without cover and it was to their credit that the soldiers lasted as long as they did. The British commander, Lieutenant General A.E. Percival and his Australian counterpart, Major General H. Gordon-Bennett, did not always work in concert, which later led to many recriminations. Although the mixed British forces outnumbered the invading army, they lacked cohesion, determination and experience. Add to this the total Japanese domination of the skies and defeat became almost inevitable.

As soon as they were organized, the 135th was sent across the causeway linking Singapore to Johore to support the 28th Indian Division about fifty miles up the west coast. When they arrived, they found that it was a lost cause, for the Japanese were pouring through great gaps in the ill-prepared defensive positions and keeping the British on the backfoot. It was during this period of the fighting that the 135th suffered its first casualties. By the 26th, it was decided to make a phased withdrawal to Singapore.

Charles and his comrades were involved in five days' of heavy rearguard action in support of the Gurkhas. Toosey would site his guns on the edge of forest clearings and as the Japanese appeared into the open from the north, they would inflict heavy losses, before pulling back to the next clearing and repeating the same tactic. Although it slowed the enemy, they never lost their forward momentum and it was clear that Johore could not be held. Like the last inch of sand leaving an hourglass, a rapid evacuation found most of the soldiers and thousands of civilians had crossed back over the narrow causeway onto Singapore island by the 31st. Once the Argyll rearguard were safely across, a naval demolition party then detonated a large charge which blew away a long section of the 1,100 yard long causeway. Any hopes that this would deter the Japanese were soon dashed.

Charles and his companions returned to their position at Nee Soon and were soon dug in to the right of the causeway and exchanging fire with the Japanese across the Johore Straits. This came to a crescendo on 5 February, when the Japanese put down a massive bombardment, to which the well-concealed 135th was able to answer with some effect. Further west of the causeway, the heavy barrage had caused some weakened Australian units to pull back, which allowed the Japanese to land. The 135th was ordered to fall back on a reserve position during which time the gap in the causeway had been bridged and the enemy began to cross. A successful counter-attack on Hill 95, overlooking the causeway was made by the 8 Indian Infantry Brigade supported by the guns of the 135th. A night withdrawal by the infantry left some of the 135th guns in danger of being surrounded and it took some heavy fighting to bring them to safety.

Charles managed to write a postcard to Louise in which he matter-of-factly describes his recent experiences. After telling her of his promotion to Battery Sergeant Major (Warrant Officer Second Class), he wrote;

> *I have sent you a cable telling you that I am safe from the recent 'Dunkirk' from the mainland in which I took part. I hope you have it and that you didn't worry too much during the news of the fighting . . . I am perfectly well except for mosquito bites and sore legs, the result of going into action in a pineapple plantation!*
>
> *What a country this is!! Pineapples growing like weeds, rubber trees everywhere, Simply enormous butterflies, ants an inch long, bananas all over the place (but not ripe at this moment) and every type and variety of wriggling and creeping creepy crawlies all of which share one's mosquito net at nightime.*
>
> *We're just going to bang off a few rounds and put some yellow gents where they belong. So, cherrio!! All my love.*

Louise did not receive this card for another four months and it was to be the last uncensored correspondence she had from Charles for three and a half years.

With the Japanese squeezing the British into a last enclave around Singapore City, it was only a matter of time before the defenders would be forced to capitulate. During these final hours of confusion, ten members of the regiment's 499 Battery were cut off and captured. Held to ransom, the Japanese demanded that the British should surrender within twenty-four hours or the prisoners would be killed. The written demand was delivered to the Royal Artillery's Divisional Command HQ and from then passed onto higher authority, never to be heard of again. When twenty-four hours had expired, the unfortunate hostages were tied to trees and shot or bayoneted. Miraculously, two managed to survive and make their escape back to their lines and report this dreadful atrocity.

Sunday, 15 February began with the 135th firing in support of the 8 Indian Brigade. Calls to replenish the dwindling supplies of ammunition were not answered until a message came that an armistice had been called and all guns and equipment should be destroyed. For the second time in two years, Charles found himself wrecking his regiment's precious weapons. Toosey then called his men together and pulled them back so they would go into captivity as a unit. Singapore had fallen in what Winston Churchill described as,*'the worst disaster and capitulation in British history'*. There were many who felt Churchill was at fault for describing Singapore as a fortress when, in fact, it was a naval base on an unfortified island with a huge civilian population.

There was a delay of two days before the regiment actually had contact with their victors. When they did appear, Charles was incredulous that such small men, who were dwarfed by their obsolete looking rifles and fixed bayonets, should have over-whelmed a numerically superior and well-equipped army. The initial behaviour towards their captives was generally correct and in some instances, affable, which was in marked contrast to the appalling orgy of killing of the Chinese population.

The British had capitulated a mere seventy days after the Japanese had invaded Malaya. This had landed the victors with the problem of what to do with the 130,000 men they had captured; something for which they had not prepared. The nearest appropriate area from the city was the barrack complex at Changi, fifteen miles up the east coast of the island. Charles wrote his second letter after he arrived in Changi;

Feb.'42

My Dearest,

Whenever POWs gather together after the war – if the war ever ends, I am sure that someone will say; 'D'you remember the walk to Changi?'

It was our first taste of Japanese unpleasantness. On the 17th at about 1 pm, we suddenly had orders to move to Changi in the North East of the Island – about 20 miles from Singapore Town. No transport, of course. Carrying all our kit, we started off from our last position soon becoming one unit in a vast procession of tired figures trudging through the tropical midday heat. Only a month off of the sea, almost entirely unclimatised, the 18th Div troops felt worse than most people. We trudged past shelled villages – Payer Libes we had ourselves shelled and turned to ashes, past bodies still laying in the roads, a defeated army in the hands of an Eastern Nation. I saw a tiny detachment of elderly RAPC (Royal Army Pay Corps) personnel. The heat – I can hardly describe it!! I have never longed as much for the milk of the green coconuts above our heads as I did then.

We arrived at Changi – Roberts Barracks – before dusk. The whole of the white troops in Singapore were concentrated here. The confusion and crowding were indescribable. The buildings had been heavily bombed and sanitation and a water supply were non-existent. The smell of the dead was everywhere. Men were told to walk to the swamps by the sea for latrine purposes, but you know what tired men are like. Before morning, excreta was everywhere. I slept on a couple of boxes. No food has been supplied by the Japanese, who seem to regard us as rather strange animals. Fortunately, we have ourselves saved rations and are now eeking them out but one feels famished.

Charles, in common with a few other prisoners, decided to keep a record of his experiences. Rather than just write a diary, he used the medium of letter writing to keep alive his connection with his new bride, Louise. He explained this in his first letter;

Changi, Roberts Barracks, Feb.'42
My Dear Wife,

I am a Prisoner of War.

On the 15th of this month, the 'invincible' city of Singapore fell after the Japanese had pounded the island for a week and shelled and bombed the city from all sides for three days. Of the battle I shall say nothing here: sufficient is it to say that I have escaped unwounded and am now a 'non-effective!'

It seems incredible that I shall be cut off from you for months – even years at the worst, God speed the Red Cross organisation – if the Japs recognise such a body, in its efforts to alleviate our lot,

I sat down to write this letter with a vague idea in my head – an idea that has now crystallised into a resolve that whatever happens, I am not going to be cut off from you. We are going to be linked together through the medium of pen and ink and pencil and paper as we always have been; we are going to continue to put our thoughts on paper. If we cannot answer each other's letters we can at least store up incidents and ideas which can be conveyed to each other in the misty future.

So long as I am able, I am going to write you at least one letter each week. The continuity of our correspondence will go on and on. One day you will read these letters . . . And know without doubt that you are with me . . . now and always.

Chapter 5

'Phoney' Captivity

A strange period of limbo followed, with the prisoners unguarded and left to organize themselves. Changi had been built to house a large peacetime army and consisted of many buildings, parade grounds and playing fields and was described as the finest British Army overseas establishment. For those who were held here, it seemed like the ideal form of captivity. The Japanese posted guards on the roads between the sprawling camps that made up the whole Changi Camp and some prisoners would not see a sign of their captors for days. This sense of unreality was further emphasized when the Japanese ordered their prisoners to erect a barbed wire perimeter fence to prevent escape, although this was not really an option. Imprisoned on an island surrounded for hundreds of miles by enemy-held territory and unable to blend in with the native population, it was little wonder that so few made the attempt.

Nearby this strange prisoner of war camp was the island's grim main prison, which later gained infamy as a squalid and overcrowded hell-hole, in which 5,000 men were crammed into an area designed for 600. It was this that gave Changi its later notoriety.

For the time being, the British had to fend for themselves, even to the extent of finding food and setting up their own hospital. Charles wrote his third letter;

Feb.'42

My Dearest,

I am sitting in a small room on the top floor of a barrack block in Changi. Outside I can see the tops of palm trees and, in the distance, the blue waters of the Straits of Johore . . . I have just seen powerful units of the Japanese fleet sail majestically up the channel to the Naval Base, at which we berthed so little time ago. A dispiriting sight . . .

Order has been restored from the chaos here. The 135 has taken over a whole block, the 499 Bty on the ground floor, the 344 on the second and ourselves, the 336, on the top. I have a room with the other two 336 Warrant Officers. We have found bedboards, so are not on the concrete.

No food from the Japanese yet. We saw Japanese soldiers after the Capitulation and saw many units including tanks and artillery on our way to Changi. There seems to be no POW administration whatsoever. We have not been counted, examined or searched. If this state of affairs existed in Europe, half of us could have escaped by now. Here we are in the midst of a native population. A European is picked up from the streets as easily as a negro in the Strand. The Japanese are said to be shooting hundreds of Chinese but so far we have escaped a like punishment for destroying our guns in contravention to orders. Maybe in the confusion of the Capitulation we shall get away with it.

We have been bathing in the sea but less and less men go as more and more display the signs of weakness. Two fainted on my parade this morning. The Army Act has been re-established. We are enforcing normal discipline and are attempting social activities – lectures, debates etc, to combat antipathy. What we want is food. We are very hungry.

Charles describes a typical daily menu;

Feb.24 Menu

Breakfast	*1 Teaspoon Sardine, 2 biscuits, 1 pint tea*
Lunch	*1 pint tea*
Evening	*Dessert spoon stew, 3 biscuits, 1 pint tea*

Charles refers to the Army Act being re-established. The senior officers felt this to be the only way to keep discipline and to prevent anarchy breaking out. Preservation of the officer – other ranks status quo led to much resentment, especially amongst the Australian prisoners, who felt the British command had forfeited any right to lofty status. Although some of the duties set by the officers were just time-filling, a proper command structure ensured that conditions in the camp generally improved. This self-regulation also had the added bonus of keeping the Japanese presence to a minimum, although this neglect was most keenly felt in the absence of any regular food supplies.

Whatever the motives of the British senior officers, their behaviour caused a huge amount of resentment amongst the men, who felt that sharing imprisonment should break down the old class system. Many officers showed arrogance and indifference by expecting preferential treatment and food. They even meted out punishments to those soldiers who contravened some petty breach of army discipline. One such punishment meant the confinement of several other ranks in a filthy wooden shed and having their already inadequate rations cut to one daily meal. The Australians were outraged, tore down the building, released the prisoners and carted off the timber for firewood.

Very soon, the starvation rations and insanitary conditions led to an inevitable increase in the numbers of sick;

My Dear,

Dysentry (sic) has arrived. The chaotic early conditions, the effects of the tropical sun upon the aftermath of war, the millions of flies, the weakened conditions of men, all have caused or helped to cause the rapid spread of disease. Men are going down with dysentry (sic) in large numbers. We are doing all that is possible with special latrines etc. I have put an all night piquet on the latrines in case men faint.

The arrival of Nippon 'food' – some sacks of rice – has caused everyone's stomachs to go out of order. At last we have the bulk – typical menu;

Breakfast:-   *Boiled rice, spoon of milk, tea*
Tiffin:-   *Boiled rice, tinned herring mixed together*
Evening:-   *Boiled rice and a little stew*

The change to Asiatic food has caused acute internal trouble. I myself am down with acute diarrhoea. I can hardly stand. Incidentally, the tropical sores with which my legs were covered at the end of the campaign have now healed up through the action of the sea water.

Officers are not allowed to wear badges of mark-just one pip on the left breast pocket. They are furious.

Some of our 'missing' and wounded have turned up. Binoculars, compasses have had to be handed in.

So many men are now sick that the whole of Roberts Barracks is to be turned into a hospital. We are to camp out on sandy ground near Changi Swamps. There is no shelter. I am now better. Your photos are a great help.

Charles kept thirteen snaps during his incarceration; all with a Japanese approval stamp on the reverse. By the time he was released, some were almost invisible with damp and wear. His army paybook was similarly stamped and gives a remarkable amount of information during his time as a POW. It lists all twenty-two protective inoculations and three vaccinations he had during captivity, including those administered by Japanese medical officers.

In tents, Changi. March '42
My Dear

We are living in tents on sandy ground near Changi Swamps. We are crowded but fairly comfortable. Things are looking up. To get away from the depressive atmosphere of the damaged barracks is a good thing. We have laid the tents out in normal lines and following a program of parades, lectures etc. Food is better but the vital vitamin B1 is sadly missing. Eat your vegetables – beri-beri is a dreadful disease!!

Typical menu – Breakfast Rice, tinned carrot, tea
Tiffin Rice, jam, coconut mixed

Evening Rice, stew, tea

We have made carts from old lorries for transport of rations, wood etc. and are building a hairdresser's shop. Canteen facilities are non-existent. Swimming is stopped. I have 97 men in my Troop. After parade, either I or the Troop Commander read to them or organise lectures. Last night I borrowed a gramophone from a sergeant in the 148 Field Regiment and gave them a recital -classical first half, dance music second half. Although our main job is, as the Colonel said at the Capitulation, to keep ourselves alive, it is up to us to keep men from sinking to the lowest levels of existence.

I am fortunate in having you behind me – always.

This relatively up-beat letter was quickly followed by a tragic postscript;

I have just seen a gunner die from dysentery and feel so upset that I feel I must say how bitter I feel against the Nips, who have caused an epidemic like this by crowding men together like cattle at the end. Once started, a thing like this is hard to stop. Warburton was quite unrecognisable. He could only have weighed six stone – just a skin covered skeleton. This is worse than dying in action. Forgive my mood.

Food became the all-consuming topic of conversation and its acquisition the greatest activity.

Dearest

A Black Market has started in the absence of canteen facilities and the non-existence of European rations. Adventurous spirits are getting through the wire (which we have ourselves put up) and are contacting Chinese who, with true commercial instinct, are charging enormous prices for tinned food. Corned beef – small tins-are about 5 Straits dollars (8/-to 10/-in Sterling), Milk is 5–6 dollars (11/-to 13/-) per small tin and so on. And yet, the craving for food is so keen that many people are only too willing to pay these prices. Bread rolls about 5" long are 1 dollar (2/4d). I have a Gunner Lloyd who has rapidly become a rich man through these activities. He is converting his stock of notes into rings etc. A dangerous game to play with the threat of shooting if caught by the Nips outside the wire.

The only conversation amongst the men is about food. The female sex has been completely ousted as a topic of conversation. Men are smoking leaves in lieu of tobacco. Some men who have been heavy drinkers are already going down with beriberi. BSM Murkin (499) died from dysentery today.

The only occasions that the Japanese made their presence felt during this strange period of unreality was when they called for the prisoners to be paraded for visiting dignitaries.

Since we became P.O.Ws, we have had to line the roads to Changi three times. On the first occasion, high Japanese Military officers inspected their 'bag', on the second it was the Jap Navy and on the third, the new civilian administration of Singapore, who lounged back in their British and American cars and stared at us. One's blood boils but anger does little good. If one were in German hands, one at least would have an organisation with which to deal. There is none here.

After about six weeks, the Japanese began to make use of the huge pool of labour they had idling away at Changi. Charles wrote his tenth letter in April;

My Dear

During the last ten days the unit has had to send a working party to Singapore each day. I went on three of these parties and thoroughly enjoyed the change. On each occasion we were transported – 50 in a small lorry from Changi Gun Park to Singapore Town at breakneck speed which seems typical of Nip driving.

My first trip was to the Docks area where we were engaged all day in unloading empty petrol drums from lorries and stacking them. The Japanese were quite friendly. It was incredible to notice the leg wear adopted – British Army gym shoes, white Indian socks – suspenders-and shorts !! The Japanese Army seems to depend upon supplies filched, stolen or won locally. Two of our men were slapped – a curious Nippon punishment – for attempting to enter a shop to buy food.

On the second trip, we went right into the docks and were forced to unload bombs from lorries and pile them by the quayside. Nip soldiers did a flourishing business by getting tins of marmalade from the ruins of a warehouse (a 'go-down') and selling them to us at a dollar each. One Japanese NCO came up to Major Banham and myself and asked where we went to school etc.

The third day saw us at the station where we piled empty petrol drums. We found a box of British Army biscuits and managed to steal most of them. They were like manna from Heaven!! I felt a new man with something solid inside me again! One's teeth are inclined to ache with such solid food however.

There are rumours that we are to move from Changi to a place called Bukit Timah, near Singapore. I should like to get out into the world again: this is like a perpetual TA Camp, with no chances to get out or satisfy one's hunger.

Never mind – we're going to have a North Cray breakfast again . . . some day!!

A few notes about conditions here.

A few cigarettes and a little soap issued by the Nips.

One can get anything for cigarettes. Am laying in privately, medical supplies and toilet requisites.

'Limed' rice issued. Many men sick.

High standard of internal organisation. Rgtl Gardens, Rgtl Educational Scheme, Changi 'University', Div 1 Concert Party. Church Parades all in being.

Organised with Bty Captain, a Battery Arts and Crafts Exhibition. Did not win prize with bamboo serviette rings. Rgtl Exhibition followed, judged by Major-General Beckwith-Smith 118 dist.

Grave problems of worn out footwear
Grave doubts about allowing of Red Cross.
No fresh vegetables. Beri-beri cases increasing.
Dysentery dying down – thank God.
Major Banham gives his WO's and Sgts a lecture on news and
memories every Weds. Very depressing.
    Regtl Diary of Action written.
    Rice grinder constructed. Rice biscuits made. Cake made
from artificial manure . . . not bad.
    Man claiming to be a Seer giving out prophecies in the
Beds/Herts Rgt. Said his CO would be in hospital in a fort-
night's time. Was punished for spreading malicious rumours,
but . . . his CO went down with dysentery.
    'Singapore Post' Foot Scabies, Tinia Ringworm increasing.
    General Heath inspected all RA units – 5th, 88th, 122nd, 135th,
137th, 148th, 155th Says the Field Artillery did magnificently
under terrible conditions. Japanese admit superiority of British
gunners, suffered heavily.
    Visited Roberts Hospital 2/5/42 to see wounded, sick etc
    Received orders to move 4/3/42. Moving on 5/5/42.

With so many men confined together, there was bound to be a wide range of skills and talents. The 'Changi University' became established and had faculties of modern languages, English Language and Literature, History, Geography, Mathematics, Economics and Theology. Each faculty had four or five lecturers offering lectures every day, as well as tutorials. The University proved very popular and helped to keep the inmates' minds off their empty stomachs.

The 18th Division even managed to form a symphony orchestra, which played prison-made instruments and were led by a former London Philharmonic musician.

The Japanese realized that the daily transporting of work parties from Changi was wasting too much time, so a number of temporary camps were built near the work sites. As Charles revealed, the 135th left on 5 May for Bukit Timah and . . .

We have arrived here after a terrible march of 26 miles in the full tropical sun. Many fell out and are still coming in. Finished, but felt pretty faint at the end. Living in damaged RAF camp.

Some 3,000 prisoners were sent to Bukit Timah, in the centre of the island to help build a Shinto shrine, named Shonan Jinjya, to commemorate the Japanese victory. It was to be constructed on a small island in the MacRitchie Reservoir on the Singapore Golf Course close to the camp, from where Charles wrote;

My Dearest

This is definitely a move for the better. We, with the rest of the 53.1.B have been installed into an ex-RAF camp – at one time Far Eastern H.Q. It consisted of attap roofed wooden bungalows on a series of hills surrounding a small valley. When we arrived, the camp was just as the fierce fighting around here had left it. Many of the bungalows are now just concrete slabs in the ground with debris upon them. Almost all huts have shell holes in the roof. A giant water tower lays where it crashed on the top of a hill and our noses tell us that there are still many unburied.

The march from Changi was a real endurance test. The Japanese brought us through almost the most crowded parts of the city of Singapore – a dreadful loss of face to ourselves and a gratifying exhibition to our captors. And yet one could see that not all the enormous Chinese population had turned against us. One fat old Chinese woman came out of a shop and, through her action, caused a galling scene. She threw the rolls to the men, who, hungry as they were, scrambled for them. A feather in the cap of the Japanese to see Englishmen scrapping in the gutters . . . The last part of the journey was hilly and caused much trouble.

However, here we are. With the other two 336 WOs, I am installed in a small room at the end of the bungalow and am having a bed made from planks. No water or sanitation, of course.

The work here is to be the construction of a Shrine to the

34

Nippon dead on a hill on the Bukit Timah Golfcourse, nearby.
The work is being designed by Nippon REs (Engineers) and
done by us.

This is known as No.2 Camp. No.1 Camp is in Adam Park,
not far away and contains Australians, Gordons, Leics and East
Surreys. No.3 is the 54 IB, Norfolks, Suffolks and 148 Field
Regt RA. There is still no POW organisation and only a Nip
RE (Engineer) Sjt is responsible for us.

I think, if more food comes, this will be a good camp.

During their efforts to make the camp habitable, some
unpleasant relics were unearthed.

Darling Wife

A most upsetting day today. A gunner came in with an AB64
(Army Book 64 – Soldier's Pay Book) *which he said he had*
found in a pipe stuck in the ground. I went and found that the
stick was stuck into a ditch partially filled in. I had two men dig
and quickly came across the remains of some poor fellow who
had been partially blown to pieces. The head was separate and
the skull quite clean, but the body had been foolishly buried in
a groundsheet and had not decomposed. We buried as many
parts as could be sorted out and held the customary service. We
buried him as I. Cambs. His hometown was in Stowmarket.
How futile war is! A simple country lad like this – his home
amid the cornfields of Suffolk, dragged to the other side of the
world, butchered, and put in a hole under rubber trees so far
and foreign from his own lovely countryside!

He was not the only one. A pile of clay on some asphalt near
the cookhouse disclosed another. Three – two British and one
Japanese – were found near the MI Room. Four in another hole,
What misery it is!

These harrowing discoveries obviously got to Charles for he,
almost desperately, feels an overwhelming desire to declare his
love and persuade himself that he will eventually be reunited
with Louise.

. . . Oh my darling, I dare hardly to open my heart to even you. Only one thing matters. I __must__ see you again. I __will__ see you again. I __will.__ __I WILL.__ Nothing is important besides that.

However black the outlook is, your memory shines through like a star . . . my guiding star, a star which will remain with me like the millions of shining specks which have shone in the tropical skies forever and forever. I love you dearly.

By the next letter, the fifteenth, Charles had regained his composure and even allowed himself a little optimism.

Dearest,

A short description of the work here.

Bukit Timah Golf Course is to be converted into a Shrine with a memorial as its focal point. A series of roads will be laid out and flowers and trees planted. Hump backed Japanese bridges will be built at three points.

For the first week we had to march long distances each way at the other end of the glorious lake – the MacRitchie Reservoir, which lays amid perfect surroundings on the golf course area. Hard to believe that one is in the tropics at first sight, so rigorously have palm etc been excluded.

The work is done Oriental fashion, that is with no mechanical aids other than spades, chunkols and baskets for carrying earth. A terrible soul destroying occupation. We are nothing better than slaves or the coolies whom you see in pictures of China.

After a week or so, the Japanese pioneers were removed and REs (Jap Army Engineers) took their place. They are a better lot. On the first day, all our officers got beaten up as a spade was missing at the end. This has not reoccurred although many men have been slapped and punched. Unfortunately, efforts to stop this are met with amazement as it is the same to the Jap Army as CB (Confined to Barracks) is to us. A Lt-Col. will slap a Major's face in front of the Troops if he wishes. One cannot help thinking of Queen Elizabeth's habit of boxing her Minister's ears!!

The men work very slowly indeed. We are taking the view that if they do not wish to work, they need not be forced to but must take the consequences from the IJA. Very unsatisfactory as some men are born workers.

The Japanese must rank among the foremost landscape gardeners in the world. The steps leading to the Shrine are granite. The bridges of teak with brass knobs.

I am glad that the IJA have put us to work because it offends no Hague Convention or Red Cross dictates. One is in the open and is hungry for even the swill which we call food. There are rumours of pay – 10c per day all ranks. A fair number of men are left in camp for Camp organisation. I take parties out about two out of three days.

Things could be a lot worse – so lets look on the sunny side!! It won't be long now.

His last upbeat comments refer to a persistent rumour that, as the Japanese could no longer feed them, the prisoners were to be sent to neutral Mozambique for repatriation. He continues in a hopeful vein with his description of Singapore and even ends with a little flirtatious teasing.

Although I have never visited Singapore Town as a free man, I have seen enough of it to be able to describe to you that famous Junction of the East.

The European part of Singapore is clustered around Raffles Square and St. Andrews Cathedral, which are near the water front. Behind this quarter, there extends for thousands and thousands of yards the native quarters, predominately Chinese. One can only liken this part of the city to a gigantic ant hill. Along each side of the streets are hung the vertical Chinese advertisements, while in narrow streets bamboo's stretch above one's head from window to window carry all the family's washing. The shops, except those in the European quarter, are open, bazaar type. The owner sits on a chair in the pavement. Under Britain, hawkers were not allowed in most main streets but now the Chinese coolies sit everywhere, chewing betel nut

and displaying their wares – perhaps a chicken or a small bunch
of onions or half a dozen pomelous. It is incredibly fascinating.
Oh my darling, how I wish I was free and had you here with
me. More and more I feel that anything done without you with
me is so much wasted.

I should like to see the Raffles Museum. I should like to go
into St.Andrews Cathedral and Raffles Hotel. I should like to
go to the famous Cabarets – the Great World, the Happy
World, the New World. Singapore was the amusement centre
of the Far East. Also, the centre for all kinds of vice, too. I have
heard some amazing stories from fellows who had been in
Singapore for long periods. From distant glimpses of the
beautiful Eurasian girls who live in such numbers in Singapore
I can quite understand the temptation!!

I should imagine that more men are unfaithful to their wives
here than anywhere in the world except Shanghai, where there
are so many White Russians. Never mind – you have no need
to worry over yours!! And I mean that.

In May, the Imperial Japanese Army started paying their
prisoners for their labour, something that would deeply involve
Charles as his years of captivity ground on.

We are going to be paid.   *Officers & WOs 25 cents*
                              Sjts & Bdrs 15 cents
                              Gunners & L/Bdrs 10 cents
WOs will now take their turn with junior officers in taking
out parties.

The Malay currency system is that which most sensible
countries have already adopted.
(Charles was an early advocate for decimalisation)
100 cents to 1 Straits Dollar (2/4d)
½ cent and 1 cents are square coins with rounded corners.
Silver 25 cents, 50 cents and 1 dollars are being withdrawn
and paper money introduced for 50 cents and 1 Dollars.

The Japanese are issuing paper money for amounts down to
1/5 cents like postage stamps and worth 1/3 farthing.

The Japanese note for 1 Dollar upwards are fairly decent productions, each featuring a tropical fruit or tree. Rather effective.

The prisoner's new found wealth could be spent at a canteen that was organized. Captain Northcote, the Adjutant, was escorted into Singapore Town once a week to purchase extra quantities of food, soap and tobacco. This combination of an improved diet and fairly easy work resulted in an improvement of the men's health.

There was another small morale boost for the 135th.

Col.Toosey has been awarded the DSO on behalf of the Regiment and on account of its behaviour in action. An emergency reward made by the Divl.Cmdr. (General Beckwith-Smith), which has pleased everyone tremendously. Probably the result of Wavell's visit to the unit during the battle.

The staple diet was rice and Charles let his opinion of this particular cereal be known.

My Own Darling,

As a rice – eater – no, not an ant-eater, but something slightly lower in scale, I am amazed at the different varieties of rice which have come our way.

To start with we had the normal polished white type, which we know in England. Then came the 'Yellow Peril', rice with lime. On objections being raised, the Nip reply was; 'Well, it's your own rice and you put lime into it'. So we did, but it wasn't meant for human consumption (condemned).

Wholemeal rice came along at Bukit Timah – rice with the husk on. Good for (Vitamin) B.1 content, but, oh, how sore on the throat!!

Rice, which when boiled becomes a gluey mass is another kind. Ketan, it is called. A more unappetising meal I cannot imagine.

Then there is broken rice or chicken rice. Very bad quality, dirty and most unpleasant but better that white polished rice.

If you ever have rice in the house when we settle down, I'll .
. . . . . you and that's a threat and a promise!

All during his imprisonment, Charles would occasionally write a list of happenings and observations. At the beginning of June he wrote;

A few notes

Australian Canteen in No.1 Camp very popular. My first egg for many months was a wonderful experience. All eggs are duck's eggs, size about European chicken's egg. Aiming at one egg per day – 10cents.

Small Regtl.Canteen opened by RQMs (Regimental Quarter Masters)

. . . . (-the swindlers). 11 June – our first Jap Roll Call. Hopeless mess-up.

Address by 'High Japanese Official'. Australians found in cinema in Singapore. Shooting threatened.

Chinese break into camp selling 5-cent cakes etc, before daybreak.

25-pdr unexploded shell found a short way from my billet.

A race-game organised by 336 Bty on Yasme (rest) day to pull in money for welfare. CWS (Charles) cashier – you bet!

Typical meal 14 June;

B. Rice, two spoons stew, tea

L. Rice, fishcake, cucumber, tea

S. Rice, rice 'meat pie', 'apple' turnover, tea, Largely rice & ersatz. I'm afraid.

Much aerial activity on part of Nips

Commission to write Regtl.Diary, if imprisonment.

Debates organised. Spoke at several.

Sjts & W.O's Mess organised. Social evenings enjoyed with Sjts from Norfolks, Cambs, Aust. Etc. Now dominoes champ.

Dates obtainable.

C.O. obtains supply of Rice Polishings (B.1 content high) from Johore Bahru. Given to cattle in peacetime. Saving us from beri-beri now. Dreadful stuff to take.

Brigadier Duke gives lecture to Offs & WOs. Say things could be worse.

Church being built – outstanding modern murals on asbestos walls.

A postscript declared;

A bad thing has happened. All senior officers over the rank of Colonel, i.e. Brigadiers and Generals are to go to Japan. Bad for us, because the higher the rank the better bargaining powers we have with the Nips.

Our CO Lt.Col.Toosey is taking over command of the Brigade. An excellent man.

The Australians had very quickly become adept in trading with the local Chinese, often braving punishment by leaving the camp to go in search of food. They were also reinforcing their reputation for indiscipline and showed scant respect particularly for British 'brass'. Brigadier C.L.B. Duke, commander of the 53 Infantry Brigade came in for special attention from the irreverent Diggers. When the Japanese held the first formal count on 11 June, the whole of the Burkit Timah camp was paraded and discipline barely maintained. As each adjutant stepped forward to report to the Brigadier and delivered a smart salute, a roar of abuse was hurled from the ranks of Australians. This was contagious and it spread to the British troops, who gave vent to their anger and frustration for the position in which they found themselves.

This near-fiasco of a parade was about the last official function that the Brigadier commanded. In the middle of June, all officers above the rank of Lieutenant Colonel were transported to Japan and within a few months, the 18th Division's commander, General Beckwith-Smith, had died of disease. The mantle of command was placed upon the shoulders of Lieutenant Colonel Toosey who succeeded as the senior British officer.

The church referred to was a little chapel named St David's, sited in an asbestos walled shed. One of the bombardiers painted the walls with grey vehicle paint and modern 'working-class' murals were added.

The relative easy time Charles and his Bukit Timah comrades were enjoying was reflected in his next few letters, where he concentrates on local colour.

Darling,

The Wayside Cook is a feature of the East, which is unknown in Europe. He, or more likely, she, carries her utensils and commodities in two baskets on the pole over her shoulder. She arrives, squats down, puts her pan on a tiny charcoal fire, cooks her rice and eatable and then waits for the first comers.

How do these people live ? They deal in such small quantities that it appears impossible that they can support themselves. One sees these cooks surrounded by their clientele, all squatting down on their haunches and shovelling food into their mouths with chop sticks. Most insanitary!

. . . I do not know very much about butterflies, but I have quickly realised that for beauty, variety and size, they are more important in Malaya than birds.

There are butterflies of every conceivable size and shape, of every colour and every combination of colours. There are little sprites which one sees as flashes of yellow and blue, there are giants which flap slowly high overhead and which resemble slow moving birds. Some are at least 10" across.

Darling, I wish you could see them – but not me!!

. . . I wonder how many letters you had from me prior to the Capitulation ? I sent off several from Singapore and also some cables but I think many must have been stopped by enemy action.

What a grand feeling it was to see your handwriting on the envelope! How good a feeling it was to write to you!! I cannot bear to think of the time which must elapse before once again we can carry on that correspondence that we value so much.

I lost my letters at the Capitulation, but I still have your photographs, grand girl!! You don't know what they mean to me . . . If only there were any hopes of getting letters from you.

Never mind – we'll stick it out.

. . . The unbelievable has happened. We have been given an opportunity to write home. I cannot express my feelings.

I thought first of being jocular with something like this:-

'I am fit and well
Don't worry over me
The rice is simply swell
I'm as happy as can be.

I'm always thinking of you,
You have my love as well,
Keep smiling, don't get blue
Keep your chin up, darling girl!'

But thought the Nips might not like it. I therefore sent the card that I hope you will receive with the next couple of months. I am not ashamed of the fact that I wrote it with your photograph open in front of me.

The prisoners were able to supplement their meagre diet by growing their own produce.

I am not called upon to go out so much now, so, with Captain Neal (Bty Capt.) and Capt. Viney (my Troop Comdr), I have started a Bty garden. It lays in the valley on what was once a football pitch. For water, we depend on the main anti-malarial rain drain which runs nearby and, for manure, upon decomposed urine.

The produce grown were bananas, tapioca, sweet potatoes, beans, pumpkins and pineapples.

The sweet potatoes are grown either for the leaves (taste like spinach) or the roots (like potatoes). It will be a long time before we get bananas or pineapples, I'm thinking.

In August, Charles wrote another of his lists, which contained the seeds of what was to come.

43

1. *Inter-Bty quizzes popular. Am captaining 83b Bty side.*
2. *Free India Movement launched in Singapore (now Syonan)*
3. *Japanese newspaper 'Syonan Times' finds its way into camp. Unadulterated bilge. How they believe it, I don't know.*
4. *Library started. Small tin shed made into replica of reading room. Excellent.*
5. *15 August. Celebration by Nips. POW organisation supposed to start.*
6. *Korean (Japanese conscripts) arrive to act as guards.*
7. *Amateur artists draw frescos on 344 Bty walls.*
8. *Jap's pay 25, 15, 10 cents to all men, plus bonus of 5 cents to those on job outside. Trouble over distribution of bonus. Finally goes to Cookhouse, extra messing.*

After six months of minimal supervision during which the British ran their own internal administration, the Japanese instituted their own organization. The guards who patrolled the Burkit Timah area were those of the 'Indian National Army', drawn from the Indian prisoners who chose to change sides. About a quarter of the captured Indians, mostly Sikhs, saw the Japanese as a means of gaining independence from their British masters and became willing collaborators and enthusiastic gaolers. For all their swagger and petty cruelties, they were the model of restraint compared with their replacements, the Koreans.

Korea was the Poland of the Far East, a buffer state between Japan and China. After her resounding victory over Russia in the war of 1905, Japan was acknowledged as the strongest military power in the Far East. Having occupied Manchuria, she further strengthened her hold on the Asian mainland by colonizing the Korean peninsular.

The native population was then subjected to decades of oppression when even its language was under threat, for the teaching of Japanese was made compulsory in schools.

The Koreans were treated with contempt by their Japanese

rulers and nowhere was this more apparent than in the army. Those Koreans inducted into the Imperial Japanese Army were regarded as auxiliaries and not even given a rank. They were treated as inferiors, so that when they were given the task of guarding the ragged and emaciated remnants of a colonial power, they found a people regarded as lower than themselves. For these illiterate and despised peasants, the opportunity to vent their anger and frustrations on helpless prisoners and, in so doing, curry favour with their Japanese superiors was too hard to resist. Put simply, the Korean guards were brutal from being brutalized.

August 42 (Letter 29)
My Dear,
   Trouble!!
   The IJA Have ordered us to sign a declaration that we will not try to escape. Where we could escape to is beside the point. The principle is the thing. We have refused

(Letter 30)
My Dearest,
   The CO has addressed the Unit. The troops left at Changi also refused to sign the no-escape declaration. After many nego-tiations, the IJA got the whole lot into a barrack square and left them in the blazing heat. They threatened to cut off hospital supplies. More important, they cut off water and refused sani-tation. After three days the place was a mass of flies, while men were going down with dysentery and sunstroke wholesale. The senior British Officer (Lieutenant-Colonel E.B. Holmes of the Manchester Regiment) then ordered all the men to sign the declaration, stating that he would place the circumstances in front of the British Government. The CO (Toosey) then ordered us to sign, which we did.
   These Nips are bad.

Charles was referring to the notorious Selerang incident, when the Japanese, under the command of Major General Fukuei, reacted to the British refusal to sign the declaration that stated:

*I, the undersigned, hereby solemnly swear on my honour that
I will not, under any circumstances, attempt escape.*

Fukuei ordered that all 15,000 prisoners be herded into the 250
x 150 yard square at Selerang Barracks. Minimum rations were
distributed; water could be obtained at just three taps and the
sanitary facilities were non-existent. Within a short time, the
packed area was as hot as a cauldron and foul with human
waste. As if to emphasize his point, Fukuei had four men, two
British and two Australians, who had attempted to escape many
months before, taken to the beach. There, in the presence of
British senior officers, the unfortunate quartet was executed by
a deliberately inept Sikh firing squad. It took several rounds
before they were finally killed. Poetic justice was enacted when
Fukuei was tried as a war criminal and more humanely executed
on the same spot in 1946.

In order to end the suffering, Lieutenant Colonel Holmes
ordered his men to sign on the understanding that it was being
done under duress. The Japanese chose to ignore this caveat in
order to end this embarrassing impasse.

*A small amount of Red Cross has arrived. A very little jam, soup
powder and about 15 toffees a man. It comes from the S.
African Red Cross with the Portugese Red Cross. A large
amount is reported to have been taken by the Nips . . .*

*On several afternoons recently I have gone for walks with
Capt. Dearden of 'F' Troop. Quite against orders, of course,
but no one seems to stop us.*

*On the last occasion we walked a long way thro' thick forests
of mighty trees along paths which wound in and out of the great
trunks and were often covered with tropical creepers. We came
out near the lakeside and then sat talking of this, that and
t'other amid the most beautiful surrounds I've ever seen.*

*Then we noticed two armed Sikh policemen watching us. We
walked back to Camp closely followed by the two bearded
horrors, who made no attempt to detain us.*

On the very next day, Capt.Dearden was out with another

officer but came back under escort with their arms tied behind their backs!

Our last walk, I'm thinking.

As the work on the Shrine neared completion, the prisoners had an increasing number of hours to idle away. Charles even had time to think about his army pay.

I wonder what is happening about my pay?

I was made up on the 31 Jan. A fortnight later, Singapore capitulated. If three weeks had elapsed, the Part II making me paid A/WOII would have been published. As it was, on the day of the Capitulation, the O.C. had the entry making me P/ALWOII put in my Pay Book. So long as I hold on to the AB64, I think things will be grand.

Sept.42
Dearest,

The Shrine is nearly finished and was dedicated yesterday. All kinds of queer rites as you can guess. Another shrine has been finished on another hilltop near the Racecourse and yet two more (one of them to the British fallen . . . much smaller) in the same neighbourhood. These people love their shrines.

The Golf Course may be spoilt for the handful who play golf but generally it must be conceded that it has been vastly improved. I hope – when we retake Singapore – that we shall leave it as it is. Lots of sailors and Japanese civilians and European neutrals visit it. I'd like you to see it . . .

I was never sure whether I was confirmed or not but as I knew you were, I have taken confirmation classes with the Padre (Adams) and today – 18 Sept'42 – was confirmed by the Bishop of Singapore in the Camp church. A moving ceremony.

With plenty of time on his hands, Charles described how the prisoners passed their time.

Letter 38

My Dearest,

In an effort to attract money for Camp purposes, the 135 has laid out a complete Race Course in the site of a ruined bungalow.

The oblong concrete patch is marked out in an oval like a cardboard table game and the horses are of metal about 3 ft long. Hedges are of bushes. There is an enclosure, stable etc. The jockeys are the small men of the unit. There is a Tote and bookies in the Ring. There is overhead electric lighting. The game is conducted by two officers who throw dice. If 3 and five turn up, No 3 horse is moved 5 paces. A Norfolk's officer does a running commentary.

The whole thing is most ingenious and exciting. The money flows in, especially from the AIF (Australians) and the Japs are spellbound. I'm afraid most of them were pulling rickshaws not long ago . . .

Quite a lot of Red Cross has arrived – all S. African. There are boots and foodstuffs in bulk – peas – malt porridge etc. We should do well for some time, I believe.

It is quite unbelievable to taste cocoa again. There are a lot of trilby hats !!

I'm afraid these good things make one very unsettled indeed. They increase our longings.

Charles put these longings into words in his next letter.

Letter 40 Oct.'42

My Dearest,

It is almost a year since I last saw you. The longest year I have ever spent . . . If it falls to my lot that I never see you again I shall be happy in my knowledge that you and I have shared a love which I think was spontaneous on both our parts, a love which was not bred among the artificial allurements of modern life but in the clean air of the countryside, not by the attractions of flattering clothes but at a time when our interests caused us to wear the simplest and most sincere garments. (a reference to their cycling club days)

If I do see you again – and I pray to God that a miracle will happen and that I shall return – our love will be so strong and we shall be bound by the ties of anxiety and care so strongly that our previous attachment must look weak by comparison. I shall and have always been true to you. I know that you are faithful to me.

All my thoughts are of you. You are to thank for a strength of mind as my parents are for my bodily strength which is going to be tested to the ultimate degree.

Meanwhile, you are carrying on in England – doing my job as well as yours. Here, in Malaya, I realise that I have a grave responsibility to the men under me. A General said just before the war that his most difficult command was as a Lt.Col. of a POW Camp in Germany in the last war. I can realise what it was like . . . My love to you.

Charles then wrote of the surrounding vegetation and tools the prisoners used.

A most amazing plant grows under the rubber trees, which surround the bungalows in the camp. In appearance it is something like a clover but its leaves are very finely cut. Nothing unusual in appearance, I can assure you.

But just touch one leaf! Instantly, the whole plant 'dies'. The flowers drop their faces to the earth, the stems sink, the leaves curl up. What has been a large patch of green and blue has turned to a dull green. I'm sure that the plant recovers. A fly will cause the phenomenon.

When one looks across the lake one sees a mighty growth of trees. One often sees monkeys swinging from branch to branch. But what takes one's eyes are the great patches of colour provided by flowering trees.

I do not know the name of these trees except the popular one of 'The Flame of the Forest'. The flowers are huge, creamy yellows as buds, turning to fiery red at maturity. Against the green of the vegetation they are a wonderful sight . . .

When we first arrived in Malaya, we met a new tool – a digging implement known as a CHUNKOL.

You see, my dear, spades are no good in a country where the peasantry doesn't wear boots! The chunkol – like a large Dutch hoe is therefore used instead.

It is raised above the head and then brought down smartly into the earth. Being non-Asiatics we have to use them. Incidentally, did you realise that all-practically all-earth moved from one place to another by the natives is carried in baskets? And now that we are on one level lower than natives, we also carry these little baskets loaded with dirt.

Soul destroying work. To think we have sunk to this!

P.S. Even more soul destroying is being in charge of a party and doing nothing all day.

Letter 44
Darling,

Personal possessions in this situation become far more valuable as each minute, day or week passes.

By personal possessions, I don't mean ordinary kit but rather the photographs, keepsakes, personal property that reminds one of something or someone at home.

My pen, for instance – and have you noticed the Quink I am still using? I have my watch and, best of all, my photographs. The pencil you bought at Annan is here with me.

I suffered a grievous loss the other day when I found that the pressed flowers from your wedding bouquet had been invaded by a tiny tropical insect and had crumbled to dust. Never mind, never mind . . .

Charles also writes of a group of fellow captives and his Japanese captors.

Letter 45
My Dear,

A rather strange section of the prisoners here are the Malayan Volunteers. In Malaya, the TA is represented by the Straits

Settlements Volunteer Force and the Federated Malay States Volunteer Force. Both are known as the 'Volunteers'. With the exception of the regular PSIs, all are businessmen, planters etc. All are older than the average. They have now the peculiar experience of being POWs in their own country. I was talking to some the other day who were working on a grass cutting fatigue for the Nip cavalry. One actually told me that on a previous day he had been set to work to cut grass from his own garden. Nip officers are now in his house. A galling experience!!

. . . One day – oh, let it be soon! – I must tell you about the following:-

2/Lt Aoki (the Sword Swallower), Sjt. Major Obara, 'Horace the Drain Man', 'Wanker' Lt. Sato, Capt. Hashimoto (who swum the Straits of Johore) and others.

The Japanese are an incredibly childlike race, vicious as a schoolboy and delighting in the torture of animals. Yet – they love flowers.

The Australians are doing well out of the petrol racket – stealing petrol and selling it through the wire to the Chinese. They sold a whole horse t'other day, getting it out of the Camp in pieces. One of my own sergeants asked for, and obtained, a daily supply of petrol for the steamroller he drives !! Incidentally, I drove this t'other afternoon. Rather amusing . . .

The Japanese officer is a funny man to Western eyes. His service dress is usually of green, altho' I have seen many variation colours between suits and even between breeches and coats.

Starting from the bottom, he wears jackboots with spurs. Into these are tucked the baggiest riding breeches ever worn by man.

His tunic is a 'Bum-freezer' and only extends to the base of his spine at the back. Under this he wears a white shirt, opened at the neck and turned back under the collar of his coat. Badges of rank on the lapels. And then his sword . . . No Nip officer is ever dressed before he buckles his sword on – the double handed curved Japanese sword with which so many Chinese are executed.

Charles writes another heartfelt and slightly desperate declaration of love to Louise:

My Darling,

Are we going to change much during these months of separation?

Say we are POW for 2 years . . . How are we going to find each other at the end? As you know, when people are together, they grow like one another. When they are apart, they tend to become like those they mix with.

We began our companionship with identical interests, feeling and background. Now we are apart, and while you are mixing with the Officer type in a civilised land, I am at the back of nowhere trying to look after men who will gradually deteriorate into little better than savages if the Japanese hold them for more than a couple of years.

When I return, shall I appear to you as an uncouth savage? Will it be fair to you to take up our life as we left it when I am different to the person you married?

Louise, whether under these conditions I become a gibbering imbecile, you can rest assured that to me you are still the most marvellous person in the world: that even if I return when you are 80 and I'm 80, I shall still think – I shall still know that you were the only girl I've ever loved or ever shall love.

I am very worried today, so you must please excuse these doubts!

While Charles was fretting in Singapore, Louise received an Army Form B.104-83A, which ended six months of speculating if she was a widow or not.

Dear Madam,

I have to inform you that a report has been received from the War Office to the effect that No.879400 W/Sgt. STEEL, Charles Wilfred, Royal Artillery (Field) is a Prisoner of War in Japanese Hands. Camp unknown.

A Charles Steel List followed.

Darling,

A POW Camp is the greatest hotbed of rumour in the world. Some are absolutely amazing. Listen to these: –

(a)   Hitler is dead
(b)   The European war is over
(c)   The Italian Fleet in Singapore
(d)   The Japanese can't feed us (Don't we know it !) and are sending us all to a neutral country.
(e)   The Japanese are sending half of us home with the rising sun tattooed on our foreheads. The other half will be killed if the former are taken in battle.
(f)   We are to build a railway from Thailand to Burma – over mountains and through swamps, a feat attempted by Great Britain but given up owing to high death rate of coolies.
(g)   We are to march to Thailand (800 miles)
(h)   Germans at Alexandria
(i)   Japanese in Australia

And so on

Most of these rumours were, indeed, wide of the mark and Charles could be forgiven for thinking that the construction of a railway though some of the worst terrain in the world would be considered one of the wildest. His last note from Bukit Timah was brief with shock.

Oct.'42
Dearest,

We are moving – believed to Thailand (Siam) to build a railway into Burma. I'm afraid most of the Red Cross stuff will have to be left behind.

Chapter 6

The Impossible Project

A legacy of British colonializm was the construction of a railway network to compensate for the almost total lack of decent roads throughout the Empire. They were a way of shortening vast distances and linking cities separated by hundreds, even thousands of miles. They were the mortar that bound together colonies like India, South Africa and Canada. It followed that the British considered a rail link between Rangoon in Burma and Singapore, via an existing line in Thailand. Twice the British explored this route, once in the 1880s and in greater detail in 1906. A survey concluded that the region's hostile environment of dense jungle covered mountains, together with one of the world's heaviest annual rainfalls, made the project very unappealing. The huge engineering difficulties and the estimated cost to lives overrode any advantage that could be gained over the existing ocean route. The project was dismissed as being impossible.

As early as 1939, the Japanese began preparing the ground to confound the sceptics and make this impossible project a reality. The original plan was to use about a 250,000 Asian labourers to construct this single-track railway. With the comparatively easy victories in Malaya, Singapore and the Dutch East Indies (Indonesia), the Japanese found themselves with a large pool of skilled, disciplined military personnel and they had no qualms about ignoring the convention that POWs should not be required to undertake work that was useful to their captors.

Between October 1943 to October 1944, approximately 60,000 Allied prisoners of war and 300,000 Asian labourers slaved in some of earth's densest jungle. Two Japanese engineering regiments totalling 12,000 men controlled the construction, often with extreme brutality and, at best, indifference to the plight of their unwilling workers. At any cost, the railway had to be completed in the time-span that Tokyo decreed, and the cost was human suffering on an horrific scale. Without the use of machinery, the POWs had to bridge rivers, build precarious trestles along dizzy ravines, hack though rock choked passes and drive piles in malarial swamps. Along its 260 mile route, approximately forty camps were constructed at intervals of five to ten miles. The first POWs from Changi were sent north to Thailand in June to construct the railway base at Nong Pladuk, consisting of workshops, stores and a large prison compound. As the need for labourers steadily increased, so the population at Changi decreased until it was regarded as a transit camp for the railway. Charles was amongst the second group, known as 'K Battalion' and whose first destination was the sprawling staging camp at Ban Pong, by the existing Thai railway.

Letter 49 Bangpong (sic), Thailand Oct.'42
Dearest,

What a journey!!

We marched to Singapore Station (FMSRly) on 22 Oct. and were loaded 27 to a steel closed railway van. We left that night and after 86 hours in the train, arrived at Bangpong (sic) about 64 kilos from Bangkok, the capital. During that time we passed through Johore, and the whole of the Malay peninsular. We had an average of under two meals of rice a day but fortunately carried some Red Cross tinned rations with us. It was an amazing experience, albeit uncomfortable. The backbone of mountains in Malaya were very impressive.

We knew when we got to Thailand by the abrupt change in

the native. In Malaya, all women are either swathed in clothes or wear Chinese trousers. Here, all females wear sarongs and little blouses. They are far more handsome in the main. Men are quite good looking and the fact that everyone wears some kind of uniform gives the country a Puritanical effect.

But oh! The sanitation, the filth and the poverty!! The dead dogs in the gutters, the naked dusky children, the appalling diseases which one can see.

I think that we shall have to be very careful in this country.

We are temporary occupants of some flooded sheds. Water is over our boot tops and one sleeps on a double platform down each side of the shed. Vermin and filth is everywhere. We feel like prisoners for the first time. Food is atrocious.

Ban Pong was an ominous introduction for conditions Charles and his fellow prisoners were to experience for the remainder of their captivity. It was dilapidated from overuse and disgustingly insanitary. Fortunately, they only spent one night there.

Tamarkan, near Kanchanaburi Nov.'42
My Dear,
We have arrived at No.1 Jungle Camp, Thailand.

It is in the jungle on the River Manam, about 4 kilos from the ancient walled town of Kamburie (sic).

We left Bangpong (sic) in lorries. It was extremely interesting to travel the 40 kilos to Kamburie (sic). Rice fields on all sides, primitive fish traps in the flooded ditches by the roads, weaver birds – and all kinds of butterflies in the air. Great banana plantations, bullock wagons, tall palm trees of many kinds and, all over, the glaring tropical sun. About the Siamese temples and buildings, I must tell you later.

Then through Kamburie, its gaol guarded by guards with blunderbusses, its prisoners shackled together, through the fascinating streets with the wooden frame buildings with open fronts piled with all kinds of merchandise.

Past Kamburie, under the trees, up a narrow path through thick vegetation to where a clearing has been made near a

mighty river, flowing rapidly between high banks. In the
clearing are 5 long huts with bamboo sleeping platforms on
each side . . . our future home. I am very tired. Even the
bamboo's seem soft after that train journey of so many hours
sitting hunched up.

Colonel Toosey, having made his protest that POWs should not
be put to this kind of work, decided to accept the inevitable but
to cut the best deal possible with the Japanese. He organized a
command structure, made sure that everyone knew their duties
and generally tried to alleviate the grim conditions in which his
troops lived. His capacity for remembering names and faces and
his jaunty carefree manner endeared him to his men. He also
made a point of being smartly turned out whenever he appeared
before his men. It was something that gave him a psychological
edge over his captors. He managed to develop a reasonable
working relationship with the Japanese senior NCOs, Sergeant
Major Saito, a strict but fair disciplinarian and RQMS Mura-
kami, who was responsible for food and canteen supplies.

The first morning, the Japanese camp commander, Lieutenant
Kosakata, called all the British officers and warrant officers to
a meeting, at which they received their work targets. This was
in marked contrast to the welcoming words delivered by the
Japanese commander to the assembled prisoners at
Tanbyuzayat camp in which he said;

> *You are the remnants of a decadent white race and fragments*
> *of a rabble army. The railway will go through even if your*
> *bodies are to be used as sleepers.*

Charles wrote;

> *On our arrival here we were paraded before the Jap CO and*
> *were told that we should have to work with the men.*
> *Col.Toosey held his tongue, but we are going to disobey this*
> *order if it is possible to get away with it.*
> *On the first day's work, I was out with a party. The river is*

an amazing spectacle. The current is very fast. There is, of course, no bridge and transport across the river is by barge towed by shallow draught launches. These launches are very fragile craft. We were carried over safely, but the men in the next launch were thrown into the water when it capsized owing to too many getting in on one side.

We are here to build a large portion of the railway, including cuttings and embankments and at least two bridges, a temporary one of wooden piles and permanent one of steel and concrete.

At the end of the day's work, everyone went into the river for washing and bathing. It was absolutely grand to be in the clear water and attempting to swim against the current. A fine sensation is to walk up-river, plunge in and swim down-stream, watching the banks rush by as the currents bears one rapidly down. I love swimming in the river. Officers and men are in the same boat. Food is really bad. Weak stew and rice three times a day. . . . It is raining steadily: the river is rising and last night swept away the small plank bridge almost completed. Great masses of vegetation and tree trunks are coming down. There is a lot of firewood about. These monsoons are most inconsiderate.

With his ever-observant eye, Charles made some sketches*;

Letter 53 Tamarkan Nov.'42
I wish I had a camera . . . but I haven't, so here's a sketch or two.
Lavatory
Two types of barges. A whole family lives under the shelter at the back of each.
Note 'eyes' to enable barge to see rocks etc.
A joss stick is often lit on the prow frighten away evil spirits.
This is a typical river launch.
The front of the platform is used for running against banks to enable passengers to disembark.

* See photo 26.

Bangkok is said to be the Venice of the East. Certainly it is in Thailand that the rivers are the highroads and the village high streets. Everything depends of the rivers – water and sanitation especially. . . .

. . . The Thai currency system is centred on the TICAL (or BAHT), worth 1/10 pre-war. It is composed of 100 STERANGS.

A five cent piece (we call sterangs cents and ticals dollars) is a small white metal coin with a hole in it. The 10-cent piece is the same, only larger.

Notes start at 50c and are issued for 1 Tical, 5,10, 20, 50, 100, 1000 Ticals.

All notes before the war were printed by De La Rue of London, but already the Thai and Japanese are printing their own – and very badly too!!

Letter 55 Nov. '42
Darling Girl,
   Notes from Tamarkan
   1.   *Canteen supplies very bad. S/Major Saito very anti-British (a somewhat different view to that expressed by Colonel Toosey.)*
   2.   *Incidents over officers refusing to work results in joint WOs' and officers' working party.*
   3.   *Line due to go through a tobacco plantation. Men drying leaves everywhere.*
   4.   *Work very hard. Mostly on task system. Do so much – then you go home. Tasks increased each day, or when finished, more added on. With the heavy manual work and swimming one gets an appetite for even the swill, which is given us. Hands like a Navvy's, sun is cruel.*
   5.   *First death in camp. Food quite insufficient.*
   6.   *One Yasme (Rest) day per week obtained.*
   7.   *RSM Coles allowed one ord.WO each day. An extra day 'in' for me about once in 10 days.*
   8.   *Pay put up. Officers monthly against their pay at home. WO's – 40 cents, NCO's – 30 cents, OR's – 25*

cents. Thanks goodness I don't smoke. All mine goes
on food.

9.   *An RA Officer hits a Nip, who struck a man. Dreadful*
trouble: gets off shooting, but is in solitary confine-
ment for a month on rice and water.
10.   *Bugs rapidly increasing in bamboo and always small*
amount of lice.
11.   *Wooden bridge piles being driven. Very heavy work*
indeed.

The camp at Tamarkan consisted of five long *attap* huts, each
packed with 300 men. The task they had been set was to
construct first a wooden and then, a little up river, a substantial
steel and concrete bridge over the River Mae Khlaung. This was
the River Kwai Bridge immortalized in David Lean's 1957 film.
The relatively easy days of Bukit Timar were fast becoming a
distant memory as they were replaced by long hours of heavy
manual labour, poor and insufficient food and the random
cruelties of their captors.

As with any large concentration of men, different opinions
and personalities led to disharmony. Some were life's skivers and
justified their lack of effort as striking a blow against the
Japanese war effort. This threw more of the burden on those
men who were natural workers and who took the pragmatic
view that they had no choice but to do as they were ordered so
they might as well take some pride in their work. Colonel
Toosey personified this latter attitude. Some accused him of
colluding too closely with the Japanese, but others recognized
that this, albeit reluctant, cooperation did prevent the worst
excesses occurring at Tamarkan that were commonplace at
other camps.

Tamarkan Dec.'42
   My Dear,
   17th December. The Kempis (IJA police) search camp. Took
my torch and . . . an egg. Obviously been reading last war secret
agent stuff as they broke open soap etc. The bastards!

Christmas is coming. The IJA have promised a day's yasme on this date and are allowing us to buy extra food etc.

Coffee vendors now infest our huts after dark with cries of 'Hot an'sweet' – (5 cents). We have recently contacted No.2 Camp at Chungkai with our working parties coming face to face with some Cambs (Cambridgeshire Rgt), when clearing the jungle a long way from the camp. They are not doing too well and many are dying.

I was swimming today when a crocodile came down stream. I didn't know it had arrived until it had passed!

The Japanese allowed both prisoners and their own men to bathe in the river, despite the presence of crocodiles. Later, this welcome recreation was forbidden when there was an outbreak of cholera at a camp further upstream.

Letter 57 Dec.'42
My Dear,

The question of escaping has been uppermost in our minds since February, but the difficulties are so great they appear insurmountable.

The Japanese have very cleverly placed the most effective barriers in the world around us. No barbed wire but instead hundreds of miles of tropical jungle between us and freedom. Most of this is bamboo jungle and quite impenetrable. Even under good conditions, malaria, cholera and dysentery are rampant in Thailand. The Japanese idea seems to be to weaken us so much that we are too weak to even think about risking the dangers of attempting to get thro' the jungle to Burma. Those who have attempted to escape – so far 4 ORs and 2 officers have been caught easily and shot here. Water in the jungle caused them to keep to the rivers. The Thais cannot be trusted and a white man in this country is as noticeable as a negro in North Cray. We've got to stick it out, dear. I am determined to come through alive. I am glad I married you because of the will power you have endowed me with. Nothing will ever be so bad as this is – nothing can be. The Japs are the lice of the

*body of civilisation. They must be exterminated. I sometimes
wish that we had died fighting at Singapore. It would be better
than this degradation and beatings up of a POW camp.*

Although Tamarkan did have a perimeter fence it was by no
means a deterrent, for many prisoners habitually left the camp
at night to trade with the local people. Like most of his fellow
POWs, Charles could only dream of escape, for the surrounding
jungle was a most effective deterrent. There were, however,
some desperate souls who were willing to take on the overwhelming odds against a successful escape.

The two officers consulted Colonel Toosey, Captain Pomeroy
of the Indian Army and Lieutenant Howard, Royal Artillery,
and he agreed to cover their absence from roll-calls for a couple
of days. Along with four other ranks, the officers easily left the
camp and divided into two parties. Out of necessity, they had to
keep close to the river, which made detection almost inevitable.

First, the four other ranks were captured after ten days and
returned to Tamarkan. Despite Toosey's pleading on their
behalf, the quartet were driven off into the jungle and shot. A
week later, the camp inmates were dismayed to see both
Pomeroy and Howard brought back to be brutally interrogated
by the *kempietai* before being sentenced to death. It was not
until after the war that it was revealed that the two officers had
been forced to dig their own graves and were then decapitated
by sword. The new camp commandant, Lieutenant Takasaki,
who had recently succeeded Kosakata, was tried and executed
as a war criminal.

Despite the shock of these executions, some attempt was made
to celebrate Christmas. In some of the camps, like Kinsaiyok,
great efforts were made to put on decent shows to the extent of
producing programmes. Shows titled *Frills and Follies, Follies
de Noel and Revue de Monde* were put on at the Scala Theatre,
Kinsaiyok and featured the Scala Ladies and Gentlemen of the
Chorus.

Christmas '42
My Dear,

   A Merry Christmas to you!!

   We have put on as good a show as possible here.

   Last night there was carol singing under a lamp and a Church Service.

   This morning, the Officers brought round that luxury – sweet coffee – at Reveille. We had a good breakfast – good to us – and at lunch time the main meal, brought and served out to the men by the WOs and Sjts. Throughout the day there were sports, a concert, football and a lucky bran-tub. I went swimming in the morning and afterwards picked some limes, which were growing wild by the river. They are very pleasant in our milkless sugarless tea.

   Everyone was very jolly, a forced jollity, which was rather pathetic. Maybe, next year !! By the way, aeroplanes believed to be Allied Bombers were heard passing over the Camp in December.

The construction of the railway had by now attracted the attention of the RAF and American Air Force and bombing by their own side became an additional hazard for the POWs to endure. In just under a year, Japanese supremacy in the air and at sea had been usurped, mainly by victories won by the United States at the Battles of Midway and Guadalcanal. The Japanese High Command recognized that she could no longer win the war but, by stubbornly defending her land conquests, she could avoid the humiliation of 'unconditional surrender'. By refusing to retreat from remote conquered countries like Burma, the Japanese sought to keep their homeland 'at arm's length' and secure from foreign invasion. This outer defensive ring meant an increase in the role of the Imperial Japanese Army.

Thousands were inducted into the army and this led to a diluting of its professionalism. There was a decline in the calibre of its officers and many were given organizational duties which were quite beyond their capabilities, which adversely affected the helpless prisoners of war. Large numbers of semi-literate

NCOs were commissioned as junior officers and many ended up in charge of prison camps, where their lack of managerial skills led to increased problems of food supply and increased ill treatment of prisoners. Standards plummeted as the bottom of the manpower barrel was scraped. Other ranks were filled with low-calibre recruits who included sociopaths, like alcoholics and the mentally disturbed, the majority of whom came from harsh impoverished backgrounds. A high proportion of these despised misfits found themselves guarding Allied prisoners of war, where they were, for the first time, in a position of authority and able to abuse their power over their helpless charges.

Chapter 7

Bridge over the River Kwai

Tamarkan January'43
My Darling,

A Happy New Year!! – and may we be reunited before the end of it!!

I have great hopes sometimes – hope springs eternal, you know. Anyway, at this season let us look at the bright side and do our best to be happy in our circumstances.

We spent most of New Year's Day on the square in the full glare of the sun – an old Nip punishment because two men got drunk on sake (smuggled in) and molested a Korean, who fired his rifle in fright.

Incidents and yet more incidents . . .

A few notes on what can be bought with our hard-earned 40c.

For most things, we rely upon the old Thai women vendors who carry baskets containing fruit, tobacco etc. near the working parties. When a sentry's back is turned, we hastily deal with these old ladies, who reap a rich harvest owing to our lack of time to bargain. Bananas cost 10c a bunch. They are not the bananas you know but a very jungle variety – most growing wild. Eggs are all duck's eggs – about the size of a European chicken egg and cost 5c. These are my chief purchases.

The old ladies also sell a large variety of 5c and 10c 'cakes', officially banned by Col.Toosey as 'Dysentery Cakes'.

A kind of acrid sugar cake made from gula (palm tree sugar) is also bought in large quantities.

In camp, when it is functioning, the Canteen sells soap (10c upwards), brown sugar (fairly reasonable) and raw peanuts, which are essential to eat because of the B1 content in the skin. We already have many beri-beri cases – an unpleasant disease, indeed. Tobacco is sold in small boxes and is known as Thai Weed. Most of the merchandise is Chinese.

Not a very interesting selection but how welcome as an addition to our meals! I usually eat rice, peanuts and sugar after each meal – till the money runs out and we plonk back on marrow water. Nevertheless, one hears about much worse conditions further up country – Kynscok (sic) (Kinsaiyok) (No.6) Camp for instance where the POWs are living on the water in which the Japs have boiled their dried fish.

The Japanese, after months of denying their captives any form of communication with their families relented for once. Some lucky prisoners did receive old correspondence that miraculously found its way into the Thai jungle. Sadly for Charles, he was not among the lucky ones. Instead, he was allowed to send an impersonal pre-printed card, which does not appear to have reached Louise. Despite the privations and suffering endured by Charles, he still found regret within himself about his elusive commission.

We are allowed to send a second postcard home – this time a proforma effort worded in Queen's English. I do hope you get it. I feel terribly guilty about the dreadful worry which I must be causing you. I also feel terribly upset that my chances of a Commission in this war have now gone.

I have learnt recently that if I had remained in the 499 Bty, I should undoubtably have been sent home on the official escape party. As it was, I was in the 366, who sent no one owing to the heavy casualties suffered and consequent lack of men. Never mind, never mind . . .

With the railway project swallowing up manpower through overwork, sickness and malnutrition, the Japanese injected into the workforce captured Dutch from the Netherlands East Indies. About 1,000 of these came under Toosey's command at Tamarkan.

> *Tamarkan January '43*
> *My Dear,*
>
> *We have recently built five new huts. These are for the Dutch troops who are being transported from Java and Sumatra.*
>
> *The Dutch have now arrived – and a peculiar assortment they are too. They all have their Eurasians with them. The result is that the whole lot look like coloured troops. Many are very elderly and men who were in the equivalent of the Home Guard. Again, the fact that a lot of the Dutch army was composed of native troops means that now they are separate, there is a preponderance of WOs and Sjts. We have a whole hut of various varieties of WOs (WO1, WO11's, Ensign officers and Adjutants).*
>
> *They are very pleasant and range from 15 to 69 years in age. Their families are in concentration camps in Java or, in some cases, in Holland. They have lost their homeland and colonies.*
>
> *Whatever happens we, at least, can be certain that our loved ones will not fall into enemy hands and who cares what happens so long as nothing ever happens to you?*

The work on the surrounding line and the temporary wooden bridge was completed, which enabled equipment and supplies to reach Tamarkan for the major project. This was the construction of the concrete and steel bridge, which was sited a few hundred yards upstream from the wooden structure.

The design of the bridge bore no resemblance to that depicted in the film. Furthermore, it did not span the River Kwai (Kwaenoi) but the River Mae Khlaung, some two miles from its junction with the Kwai.

Ten concrete piers were to support eleven 20-metre steel spans, which gave length of 238 metres. To allow for high water during the monsoon season, a further nineteen 5-metre wooden trusses were constructed on the northern bank, which was prone to flooding. The steel trusses were plundered from Dutch railway stores in Java and arrived at Tamarkan along with an ancient excavator and other heavy equipment. The Japanese were entirely ill equipped to undertake this hugely demanding engineering project. Lack of rails necessitated the ripping up of over 300 miles of track in Malaya, as well, as the confiscation of a third of that country's locomotives and half of its wagons. This grave shortage in Malaya led to a knock-on effect as rolling stock was replaced by material transferred from Java.

Lacking modern machinery, the construction of the piers was a serious engineering problem. Firstly a circular cofferdam was built where each pier was to be sited and filled with earth until the water had been forced out. Then a large concrete ring, which had been cast on site, was lifted into the coffer dam and the earth removed from its centre. The weight of the concrete ring helped it to sink and, with each additional ring, it finally settled on the riverbed, which, below a couple of metres of silt, was slate.

This was a delicate and difficult operation even with sophisticated equipment. Instead, the POWs had to perform virtually every operation by hand, an arduous and dangerous occupation even for the well-fed and physically robust, let alone weak and semi-starved men. With thousands of half naked emaciated prisoners climbing the flimsy bamboo scaffolding and ramps and carrying away baskets of mud and earth, the scene resembled something out of a Hollywood biblical epic.

Tamarkan January '42
My Dearest,
The concrete pillars are now sunk in the bed of the river. Gangs are working in three shifts – two gangs to a pillar, with a Nip officer or WO in charge of each. I have one of these gangs and am, comparatively speaking, quite happy at the job.
The work is hard but as it isn't general labouring but rather something at which a man can take an interest, the men prefer it. My gang, ten gunners and PO Sjts are engaged in working

the excavator. The pillar is sinking below us the whole time. Sometimes one can feel it move!! Practically all the tools are British or USA – the Nips have simply nothing of their own.

The sun is our worst enemy: it really is terrible.

Charles wrote another wistful letter on the 18 January, the only one he specifically dated.

My Dear

Two years ago we were married today.

A year ago, I slept in long grass in a rubber plantation in Johore and got bitten to pieces in the absence of a mosquito net. I remember thinking of the difference to the twelve months previously, because, after all, a man's wedding day is a really great landmark in his life. In place of the snow covered houses and church at North Cray were the raised houses of the Malays, instead of the white fields and woods were the mysterious greens of the jungle and the orderly lines of rubber trees. In place of that deathly silence of a snow covered world, there came to my ears the million chirpings and cries of Johore: and the brilliant sun and blue skies of Malaya were quite different from the kindly grey skies of Kent.

And now, this year, I am in Thailand, hoping against hope that next year I shall be back with you. Nothing will ever matter again if only I can see you again and hold you in my arms. My dreams are, quite truthfully, of you. I wake sometimes with the illusion that you are with me. I love you very much indeed, Louise.

The Japanese had turned a blind eye to the trading that went on between the prisoners and the locals, which was the only way that the inadequate diet could be supplemented. Then, on a whim, it was decided to forbid all contact with local Thais. This resulted in the prisoners risking punishment by smuggling in the badly needed eggs.

My Darling,

I was involved in a man's beating up today, which rather annoyed me. The Canteen is being so messed about, that the regular supplies of eggs are non-existent. This is about the only thing we can feed the really sick on, so we were asked to smuggle eggs into the camp for hospital purposes.

Unfortunately, we have recently been forbidden to speak to Thais. The Japs got wind that eggs were coming in so searched all working parties. The officer I was with had his glasses smashed, but I got mine off in time!!

Our turn will come . . . .

The river was the artery that fed this incredible project. There was a constant traffic of Thai river craft putt-putting their way up and down the stream and stopping off to trade with the Japanese and the prisoners. One of the biggest contractors was Boon Pong, who established contact with Colonel Toosey and between them they managed to smuggle much needed drugs and food into the camps. Boon Pong took a great risk in helping the POWs and even extended credit to his impoverished customers. His bravery was recognized after the war with the award of the George Medal by the British and the Order of Orange-Nassau by the Dutch. In a more practical way after Boon Pong fell on hard times, £40,000 was raised by an appeal by the 18th Division Association.

Letter 67 Tamarkan February'43
Happy Birthday, Darling!!
My Dear,

The rail-laying party, which started from Nongpladuc Camp near Bangpong, has reached here and the lines are now past the Camp and over the wooden bridge. Trains of diesel lorries and special wagons are already going up, while many carry Nip troops on their way to their deaths (we hope) in Burma. We are still engaged on the big steel and concrete bridge, which will take the place of the wooden bridge . . . .

I wonder if people at home realise that the adage that in the

*tropics Europeans should rest during the burning afternoon
hours is now being refuted?*

*We have now worked regularly all day, almost everyday for
a year. We are almost as black as niggers. Many haven't even got
hats, let alone shirts. An increasing number now go barefoot,
and this on stony ground, where a favourite Nip punishment is
to make an offender kneel or lie down to produce burns on his
back or knees. I wonder if we shall ever be civilised again?*

The frequent heavy rains caused landslips that undermined the
rail bed along the route. It was to one of these trouble spots that
Charles was sent.

Ban Pong March '43
Darling,

A surprise.

*Two days ago I was sent here with an RA Lt. and fifty men.
We are forming a working party for some Nip Army Engineers,
who are straightening the line after a tropical downpour had
caused it to sink in some places. We are living in huts near a
Thai temple. The advantage of a small party like this is that if
the Nips are decent – these are very good – one has a fairly
decent time. The Nip officer here speaks English and is very
polite and does his best for us. We have no one from the POW
administration . Consequently, we are allowed to deal with the
Thais etc. We are getting food from the Nongpladuc POW
Camp nearby. I cannot understand why we don't sleep there
but am glad we're where we are . . . .*

*A lot of Dutch and US troops are coming through Thailand
en route to working camps up country. They have stacks of kit
and are only too anxious to sell it for Thai currency. We 'old
hands' are buying it cheaply and then flogging it to friendly
Thais at night. No one goes to bed until about 2am and we
haven't been caught yet.*

*Even the rice sacks, which the Dutch leave behind, bring a
dollar each. Mr. Wilkinson* (Lieutenant Wilkinson was a former
sergeant major and described by a fellow officer as prickly but
a tower of strength in a tight corner) *is busy buying watches and*

as busily selling them the next day. This is a stroke of luck. The biggest we've had. We're in the money – and that means food!

This relatively tranquil interlude gave Charles pause to look about and describe his surroundings.

The Siamese temple is a peculiar building, with either walls or open sides. At one end sits a Buddha. The priests wear brilliant yellow robes and are known as 'the Mustard Club Boys'. I shall try to draw one of these temples, which are surrounded by monuments and graves.

The horns on the ends of the roof are to prevent demons from sliding along them. Practically all buildings in Thailand have these. The roofs are usually covered with glazed tiles in bright colours. All around the temples are great trees and shady walks. The tombs, or are they just memorials? – are pointed in the traditional Siamese style – and out as high as a man.

Each part is brilliantly coloured in reds, yellows and blues.

Life in the temple is not so secluded as in European monasteries. Of course, many of the priests are professional, life long, priests but the rank and file are made up of lay men. All males in Thailand serve as priests or novices for some period during their lives when it is most convenient for them. They are not paid but depend upon charity for food. Every morning, a troop of the yellow gowned figures leave the temple and, armed with pots and pans, baskets and bags, go the round of the markets and streets collecting donations in kind from the inhabitants. Rice from one, bananas from another, tea from a third. If they get a lot, they feed well – if not, they don't, but I haven't seen many starved priests about.

They have a band which is played during services but I cannot describe the din as tuneful. No instruments (all cymbals, drums and trumpets) seems in time or not with the others. It really is discordant in the extreme.

There seems to be a similar order for women Buddhists, but these are few and far between. They shave their heads and wear white robes and are most unattractive.

This relatively pleasant month-long break from the everyday misery of camp life came to an end, but not before Charles suffered another crushing disappointment.

My Dearest,

I am in a fever of anticipation. We hear that the impossible has happened and some mail from home has arrived at the Nong Pladuk Camp. Officers from Tamarkan have gone there to get those for the Camp. We are trying to get ours from Nong Pladuk.

There must be, there will be, just one letter from you. This is all I want. Just one letter from you. Oh God, I must hear from you, after these 18 weary months' silence.

Charles could barely conceal his despair in his next letter.

The mail has been dished out but I feel sure that some has gone astray. Practically all the 50 men had one or two – some six, but neither Lt. Wilkinson nor myself were fortunate. He was furious; I just dazed with disappointment. I was just shocked into silence. It is just like having a plank removed from one's feet.

Wilky (the Lt.) swears most terribly about his wife and is going to be most violent when he gets home if he finds she isn't troubling to write. I can't believe this of you.

Of course, what troubles me is the question of bombing. If I heard that you had died or been killed, I shouldn't return home: there wouldn't be any point in it.

I feel right at the bottom of the world today, so won't write anymore.

Charles, Lieutenant Wilkinson and the work party were sent back to Tamarkan at the beginning of April.

Back to Tamarkan, to find everyone with four or five letters, but none for me.

73

There are rumours of a general move up country, as the big bridge is almost finished and trains passing through OK. The rumour says that the Nips are behind schedule in the No.6 area (Kinsaiyok – in the range of mountains this side of the Burma border), owing to the difficult country and numbers of prisoners dying.

Many badly sick POWs are coming down country in lorries, many dying on the way. Some died at this camp today and were buried in our rapidly growing cemetery. The ulcers are terrible – great wounds reaching to the bone. An enormous amount of dysentery and malaria, too. This is where we are going. A happy time will, apparently, be had by all.

With the completion of the great bridge over the Kwae Yai, Tamarkan's function changed from being a workforce camp to a base hospital. Colonel Toosey was ordered to remain with just a few of his men to help organize the camp to accept the increasing numbers of sick prisoners arriving from the camps up country. Before the Tamarkan workforce was dispersed amongst the other camps, they received a copy of a letter of thanks from the Japanese, which managed to combine both a sense of unreality and self-delusion.

TO ALL ENGLISH AND DUTCH

Since coming here for the construction of the MEKURON BRIDGE, all men have worked very hard, day or night, rain or fine, through scorching heat, mastering every difficulty and have obeyed Japanese orders.

I am very satisfied with the result achieved. I now give a letter of thanks to all men for their work.

Take good care of yourselves and keep your chins up. And I hope you will return to our camp safe and in good spirits.

And I pray to God for the sake of all men.

Like all his comrades, Charles dismissed this as '*Nippon Nonsense*'.

74

Chapter 8

'Speedo'

With the worsening strategic situation in Burma, the High Command in Tokyo were forced to shorten the construction time by four months. A frantic period known on the Railway as 'speedo' caused a leap in the death rate and a huge increase in sickness. Such was the pressure put on the Japanese engineers to complete the project ahead of the original target, that prisoners were subjected to the most appalling treatment just to meet the new deadline.

Sickness was no longer tolerated and men who could barely stand were kicked and beaten until they either died or attempted to carry on working. Monsoon rains and a reduction of rations further debilitated the already starving prisoners and medicines had all but been exhausted.

Charles was sent up the line just before this panic was inflicted upon the prisoners.

Arrow Hill May'43
My Dearest,
 A short note while I am lying down. We left Tamarkan on the first of the month. A train stopped and we had to climb onto the trucks loaded with railway lines – red hot with the sun. It was a terrifying experience gripping the lines, which shifted as the train jerked over the roughly laid lines.
 At Wunberg, the train stopped for hours and a terrible

thunderstorm burst, drenching us all in a few minutes. It poured for ages and at the end turned cold. The train travelled all night with us shivering with cold and wet, hanging onto the wet rails in the darkness.

At about 2am it stopped and we got off and were told to lay down by the track. It rained and we tried to light fires to dry ourselves. I was detailed by Capt.Keane (OC Party) to

take about 50 men at 4am to the camp near the river to get breakfast, which the IJA said had been laid on. It was dread-fully hard finding people in the darkness, worst still finding the camp in the jungle and disappointing to find that they knew nothing about us when we got there. This is a common occur-rence with IJA arrangements.

I got some rice from the Nips and about 20 of us cooked a plain rice breakfast for the four hundred or so men. We finished about 10am. I went to the river and washing and and am now resting before lunch, which I believe is going to start.

Arrow Hill (Arohuil) was the extent that the Japanese trans-ported their prisoners. From now on Charles and his comrades had to endure a gruelling five day march until they reached their destination at Kinsaiyok, 117 kilometres distant.

We started the march from Arrow Hill at midday. The route was along the track and the going was terribly hard. We were carrying all we possessed plus cookhouse utensils. The heat was terrific. In places one could only walk from one sleeper to sleeper and at others along narrow tracks.

At Wampo, we crossed an amazing bridge, which carries the rails above a bend in the river along the face of precipitous cliffs. The whole thing is of wood!! And very high.

The Wampo Viaduct was a rickerty structure that defied gravity as it clung to the sides of the high cliffs above the river and was one of the most difficult tasks that the prisoners had to complete. Indeed, its construction had cost many lives and the marching prisoners were glad to leave it behind. Incredibly, it is still in use although concrete bases have been added.

We saw many parties of POWs, who seemed also too weary to greet us. The Koreans followed in the rear, making the POWs carry their kit and urging more speed. I saw one officer sit down, only to be attacked by a guard with his rifle butt. These Koreans are devils!

Some men fell unconscious with heat stroke and will, I hope, be looked after by local POWs. I sat down once and couldn't get up again owing to cramp but the MO, with whom I was sitting gave me a saline solution and put it right.

We got to Tarsao at about 11pm, after 11 hours march of 25 kilometres. I was almost completely exhausted. Many men drank river water – terribly dangerous thing to do. We were given rice and two small pieces of cucumber. People simply couldn't touch it. The four hundred men were given 2 tents to hold 10 men each.

The second day's march was along the road that the Nips used to get into Burma. Our blistered feet were very unhappy at first. At Tonchan Camp, the local POWs, themselves in a miserable condition, gave us tea to drink.

We finished our tramp at a camp, where many men were stood to attention because they got water from a spring before the Japs. Dried vegetables – like seaweed and with a bitter taste – to eat, if one could.

The third day's march took us to a camp in a swampy area on the edge of jungle. Men had to stay up all night instead of resting to keep up fires because the Nips were frightened of wild animals.

The fourth day's march took us to an Australian Camp (Kanu), where remarkable strides had been made with bamboo pipes. They had tapped a stream and conveyed water by pipes all over the camp. Here many men were sick but only ulcer cases were allowed to stay in by the IJA. Many talk of brutalities at all the camps. It rained here and we got wet.

The fifth day's march brought us to Kinsaiyok (Banyan Tree), 170 kilometres from Ban Pong, in mountainous jungle covered country, through which the river twists and turns with treacherous currents. There was no accommodation and I am *sleeping under the Dutch dysentery hospital on the ground.*

We were allowed no rest, but went out to work on the day following arrival.

Despite the beauty of the surrounding countryside, the conditions at Kinsaiyok Camp came hard on Charles and his comrades after the organization and comparative orderliness of Tamarkan.

Notes from Kinsaiyok May'43

Now in a hut – but all huts are rotten and have collapsed, so that the eaves rest on the ground. Have to stoop to get in.

Next hut (used as a transit hut) in deplorable state. Loads of mice, excreta, old worn-out boots all over the place.

No POW administration in this Camp. IJA take all men out on work. Chase out sick with bamboos quite often. No hospital recognised. MO made to carry rice only yesterday. Capt. Keane beaten up when protesting.

Food beyond belief:

> *Breakfast; Rice, dried veg. ½ pt.river water.*
> *Lunch; Rice, ½ inch square dried fish*
> *Dinner; Rice, pumpkin stew or dried veg. ½ pt river water.*

Men going down with the squitters very rapidly. Fly infection probably to blame. Work is drilling rocks with drill and hammer; then clearing rock after blasting. The Nips are devils incarnate!!

We rise in the dark, 'eat' and go on parade in the dark, squelch through the mud to work, work all day, get back in the dark and sleep the sleep of the dead.

This is a terrible place.

May'43

My Dear,

We are not allowed in the river to wash, but wash under a waterfall which enters the river some ½ mile from Camp.

The Japanese here are most unpleasant. Although some are

old acquaintances from Tamarkan, they have all changed for the worst. We hear them at night-time listening to pep and propaganda speeches by Officers, who have their naked swords over their heads.

The situation is that the schedule is behind in this area, but nevertheless the railway must be got through in time. If you saw the country, you'd never believe that any railway would get through. Roughly speaking, the normal situation is that the river is in a deep, steep valley of rocks. The railway has to cling to the face of these rocks and follow the line of the river. (A similar story to the Wampo Viaduct).

All the work is hammering drills into the rock in order to lay charges which blasts away the rock. Then there is the task of carting the rock away. There are many long viaducts to be built – these are being built of wood straight out of the jungle. Cutting these trees down and dragging them out is the worst and most arduous job of all. There are Thais working with elephants, but we do it by sheer manpower and the sting of bamboo on one's shoulders. The Thais will not allow their elephants to work too hard. <u>We</u> have no protection society. The last line of 'Rule Britannia', will get a rude reception next time we hear it . . .

I am down with my first attack of malaria. Not too severe, but sufficiently unpleasant. I had dengue fever at Bukit Timah. The Japs had us out today carrying rice. One goes into hospital with malaria in a normal country and has about a month's convalescence!!

At the end of May, the Japanese sent out work parties to those parts of the line where there were smaller but vital obstacles to overcome. Charles was one to be sent up the line to endure even greater privations. His letters begin to reflect his despair of ever returning home as he descends into the low-point of his captivity.

I am going with one of our Subalterns and about 40 men, besides men of other units to a jungle camp about 12 kilos down the river (he meant up the river) to begin work on another Section. There is no road there, and we shall be supplied by river, getting there by jungle path. Maybe it will be better than here. About 3 men are dying . . .

158 km Camp June'43
My Dearest,

The journey here wasn't bad, not being on (rail) tracks. We wended in single file through thick bamboo jungle. Plenty of monkeys. The camp, being a temporary one, is tented and being new, still clean. We are terribly crowded and I am sleeping 18 to a tent with the officers.

Again, here, the work is terribly hard and the Nips are swines, although one gunza – Sgt.Angells – who I knew in Tamarkan, isn't bad. The main job is filling in a tremendous gap with rock to form a platform for the rails. One can't imagine it ever being filled in – not by human labour, anyway.

Food is even worse.   Breakfast: Rice and water
                            Dinner: Rice, dried fish and water
                            Evening: Rice, dried veg.

It is difficult to get to the river here. I am glad I am with the officers here. Our morale is high, even if our bodies show signs of going home. It is difficult to think of a future under these conditions. My boots are almost finished.

Letter 90 158 km Camp June'43

I am not writing so much, as conditions are so miserable that they will undoubtedly reflect in these letters and that's not much good.

Apart from the malnutrition, our chief trouble is the cold and rain. We are in the tropics but the nights are very cold at this height. We are continually working in the rain and so all are suffering from the squitters. I have had acute diarrhoea now ever since early May. A kind of colic, I suppose. We have no remedy. Our only MO has been sent back to Kinsaiyok by the Japanese because he certified too many men as being sick! Now, *everyone hobbles out and only those unconscious or dying can stop in. The Camp is in a terrible mess as everyone has the squitters and usually can't get to the latrines at night in the rain. The tents leak like sieves. I believe some of us may move soon.*

Charles was right about a change of location, for on 23 June he was marched just four kilometres downstream to a fresh camp.

154 km Camp June'43
We have just marched the 4km here and have cleared jungle in order to put up the tents. The Koreans kept us at work until it was dark, so you can guess the mess in the darkness in putting up tents. I feel decidedly unwell, but have been working cutting big bamboos in the jungle.

Charles's healthy pre-war life style had served him well during his captivity and he had withstood the heavy labour and starvation diet better than most, but even the most robust of men had their limit of endurance. Charles had reached his.

My Dearest Wife,
This is a mess!!
A few days after writing the above, I came out in blisters all over and especially under the armpits. These burst and formed into running sores. The pain is intense, because both my armpits are masses of congealed pus and hair, which gets stiff if my arms stop in any one position. I have to keep my arms over my head during the night to stop my arms sticking to my body. I'm flush all over. I am using a vest – a kind of all-over bandage. I've never known anything so painful. Sgt.Pleasaunce is in the same condition.
Medical Orderly – a Pte-says that it is just a Deficiency Disease and there is nothing to be done except keep the sores antiseptic. The only bright spot is that the Nip captain in charge of the Camp is dead scared of us and won't come near us!
Oh my God!! What have we done to deserve this?

With conditions reaching a new low, it was almost inevitable that cholera, that most virulent and dreaded of diseases, should break out along the string of slave camps.

> *Sores drying up, I'm pleased to report. I have never felt so tired in my life. I am now doing CSM (Company Sergeant Major) of No. 2 Coy (OC Capt.Cooke of the Norfolks). It was about time someone was allowed to do administration.*
>
> *The dreaded cholera has broken out at Kinsaiyok. I pray to God it will not reach here. We are boiling a four gallon tin of water for each tent, so that men may wash in safety, although it gets thick after 20 men have been through it. Nevertheless, the Coy Cmdr and myself cannot boil bigger quantities as we have few cans and the water has to be carried up the cliff face from the river. The other companies are not washing.*
>
> *The 'Mad Captain' in charge of the Camp has allowed us to form a small group Administration – Maj.Roberts RA, is the CO, Lt.Primrose of the Argylls the Adjutant and CSM Knight the RSM.*
>
> *I am sleeping next to Lt.Primrose, who I'd like you to meet. He is a terrific fellow, at Least 6ft 6" and broad in proportion, with a perfect 'baby' face. He lives in London and was a sergeant in the London Scottish before becoming an officer. Like all Argyll officers, he is breezy and adopts the colonial type of discipline towards the OR's. No one would guess he was an officer. He did extremely well in Malaya, twice having bullets pass through his helmet. He was finally captured up country while unconscious after hand to hand wrestling with a Nip patrol. He was tied to a lamp post at Taipong and urinated on by all the Nips who came along. He is a grand fellow, completely fearless, also absolutely irresponsible. He tells me some amusing stories of his girl friends. He is a grand fellow to have here in these circumstances.*

Despite the efforts of Charles and his fellow officers and NCO's, cholera reached Camp 154. Charles's new friend, Lieutenant Primrose, became involved in a dramatic moral dilemma which ended in tragedy.

The worst has happened. Yesterday, the Nips were imbeciles enough to send us a new company of men from Kinsaiyok. Today, one man was dying of cholera. A Japanese officer, hearing about this, ordered the Koreans to shoot the man. Major Roberts and Lt.Primrose objected violently, but the Koreans took aim. Lt.Primrose then took the rifle from the Koreans and said he would rather shoot the fellow himself, because the Japs and Koreans would not go near the man because of their fear of infection. They were trembling with fear, although wearing face pads. Cholera is the fastest and most deadly disease in the world. Lt.Primrose shot him under protest.

Many men are dying at Kinsaiyok. One gunner in my Bty was well at 9pm and dead at 3am. One cannot bury these men for fear of soil and water infection. All have to be burnt, difficult because the IJA won't give enough petrol for the purpose.

The outlook is not very bright, my dear. I wonder who will be next. I wonder who will come through these hazards.

There then followed something that appeared at the time to be of little consequence, but would later evolve into one of the great money-making scams perpetrated against the Japanese. For Charles, it was a way of using his numeracy skills and a quiet way of waging war against his hated captors.

Letter 96 154 Camp July'43
  My Dear,
  It's an ill wind . . . From 1 July, the IJA required a new proforma for pay claims – as complicated as only Jap forms can be. CSM Knight simply couldn't cope, so Lt.Primrose has offered me the job of RSM. I took it and was immediately involved in a terrible argument with Knight, who is of the old type of Regular, with about 30 years service. He accused Mr.Primrose and myself of being TA (true) and working him out of his job. Nevertheless, he wouldn't carry on with the job. One of his own Regular Gordon Officers told him he was behaving like a 'hysterical housemaid', which didn't please him much.
  However, I am now installed in a tent with Mr.Primrose and

a runner, opposite the Nip tent. Loads of room – enough to put up a mosquito net – and now have over 600 men of every unit, colour and of 4 nationalities to look after, including one whole Company isolated with cholera cases.

Latrines to arrange, cookhouse, MI room – lots to do . . . and all day the Koreans shouting for Jeuni (RSM) Sti (the nearest to Steel they can get). The chief Korean is Esourau – not a bad little fellow.

In the morning, I get the pay claims from the Coys and consolidate them onto the big IJA Pay form. Then in the evening comes the battle with the Nips over the next days avail-ability. An enormous number of men are really sick, but still on their feet. I am not getting specialist's rates – 50c a day!!

With 'speedo' increasingly being enforced with greater brutality, the railway line was approaching completion in Charles's section.

My Dear,
Work outside is speeding up to a frenzy. The Japs are simply going crazy, as a rail gang approaches from the south-east and the track is not ready. Men are taking terrific beatings. The rail should be through tomorrow night – I have been told to have five meals ready in the next 24 hour but have received no extra rations. We had a bag of fish yesterday, which consisted entirely of fish bones. The pumpkins are crawling with worms.

Charles then had a welcome break from the misery of the camp when he was sent upstream to collect the prisoners' pay.

I have just returned from a two-day journey on my own. The day before yesterday, Esou (the head Korean guard) told me I was to go to Kinsaiyok by launch to get the pay. With a blanket under my arm and mess tins in the other, I got with him and two Thais into a launch and then sat back and enjoyed a unique journey of about six hours, as the launch battled against strong currents up to Kinsaiyok.

At places, the river was in flood and one could see masses of swirling water for miles: at others, great cliffs hemmed in the river and the launch made hardly any headward against the swirling current. I thought we should capsize – but didn't. It was a most amazing experience. The only signs of life were at isolated kampongs at the water's edge or on moored barges.

I collected the pay at Kinsaiyok after an interview with Lt.Zauki – the Camp Cmdr and travelled down stream in a barge today. I was back in about two hours. At times the barge was swirled in front of the launch by the fierce current. Hardly the Serpentine!! PS 'Did' the Japs for 120 dollars!! Paid out 20 cents a man!!

Charles's robust health began to decline as Camp 154 was evacuated.

Letter 99 154 Camp July'43
My Dear,
I am feeling decidedly on the downgrade. I have now had acute diarrhoea for three months and it is telling in increased weakness and thinness. We are to march to Kinsaiyok in a few days . . .

Letter 100 Kinsaiyok July '43
We have arrived back at Kinsaiyok. I just about made it. We now find that all fit men are to be marched further up country still. The Adjutant here, Capt.Janis, has asked me to do RSM in place of a Cambs. Sjt.Major, who seems dead on his feet. I have done so, but feel more like curling up myself.

These are bad times for us. There is a cholera 'hospital' here, but really it is a dying hut as there isn't any real treatment. Jap, Thai, British, Dutch and Tamils (male and female) are lying next to each other and magnificent work is being done by RAMC orderlies under atrocious conditions. The Japs are inoculating everyone.

The other day, four men were detailed to carry a sick man to this hospital. When they got there, the Jap there made them burn a dead Tamil woman. They themselves were dead by that night, which shows you how contagious it is . . .

The IJA are sending a certain number of sick down country and, having been examined innumerable times by both our MOs and the Japs, I am one of those to go back. The ones called fit are to march further up-country. Already some parties have left here by barge for camps down country. I shall be on the last party.

Charles and his comrades had been marched up the line to Kinsaiyok and separated into two groups. If being sick could be described as lucky, then the normally fit Charles Steel was fortunate that his health hit its lowest ebb at this moment. Instead of marching off to another primitive camp deeper in the highlands, he was to be evacuated with the many sick to larger and comparatively better-organized camps in the south. Although hard labour was at an end for Charles, the misery continued.

Letter 102 Wang Yai Aug'43
The last few days at Kinsaiyok were most unpleasant. The Japs took every fit man and left the sick to look after themselves. We were forced to get sick men out of bed to do the cooking and other jobs. Men who couldn't walk had to sit peeling onions. Sick drifted back from the march up-country, too. Some of the bullocks, which were accompanying the party came back too. It is raining heavily.

I finally left Kinsaiyok on 6 Aug, after we had completely burnt one hut on the cookhouse fire. One man died as we lifted him to put him on the barge. We made stretchers out of bed bamboos. We had to carry those too weak to walk.

We arrived in two parties at Tha Soe (sic) and there was trouble because a Korean with us couldn't find the rest of the party, which had been landed by the Thai boatman further away. That party were picked up by a Korean, who beat them mercilessly because he hadn't been able to find them in the dark.

86

We marched to Wang Yai, where we were given two tents for the hundreds of men. On the next day, we were put in and taken out of a train about a dozen times and have returned to the two tents and have apparently been completely forgotten. We have had no food issued for three days, but I am getting a half-pint rice and half-pint meat water three times a day from a friendly POW cookhouse nearby. There is a rumour that we may proceed down country tomorrow.

Finally, Charles was carried on the railway he had helped to build and arrived at Chungkai, not far from his old camp at Tamarkan.

We have arrived by railway. At last we are back in 'civilisation', as represented by a 'hospital camp' – even if the Nips don't issue medicines.

Here at Chungkai we are isolated outside the main camp. I have about 100 men of all units, Services and nationalities. Food is grand after the up-country stuff. I have bought a pair of boots. Being barefoot is the worst experience one can have.

There is a strong police force here to deal with the thieving one gets in a camp, where people aren't paid. There is a very good canteen, but the hospital is a charnel house and the average deaths are about 6 – 10 per day.

Some parties evacuated from up-country arrive by barge with sick men drowned in the bilge water at the bottom. There are a lot of amputations owing to enormous tropical ulcers.

Breakfast: *Rice, porridge, sugar (plus 5c marmalade)*
Lunch: *Tea, rice, good stew (plus 5c soya beans)*
Dinner: *Tea, rice, good stew,"meat cup" sweet gulo djapathy.*

This is good after the up-country starvation. I can eat two whole mess tins of rice, when I can get hold of it and am rapidly filling out again.

It is Sunday again. Up-country, time was not marked by events with which we are accustomed to mark the passage of time. There were no Sundays at all. No rest days – nothing but work.

Now, here at Chungkai, one is slipping back to a life where Sunday is observed, where one washes and shaves extra early, where one puts on one's 'best' clothes. There is a stillness in the air that comes on Sundays in England. It is Sunday again.

This brief interlude of tranquility was ended by a jolt of tragedy.

RSM Coles – our RSM – was brought in from up country yesterday and died today 19/8/43. I was with him almost until the end, when he lapsed into unconsciousness. I was the senior NCO here, so had to arrange things. The funeral was one of several and as decent as we could make it. I found enough 135 sergeants as bearers. Just as the funeral was about to start, a new sick party came in. Included in it was the RSM's stepson. An unpleasant shock for him.

For Charles, construction work on the railway had ended. In an incredibly short period, just one year, the two lines were joined. In a ceremony at Konkorta on 17 October 1943, a golden nail should have been hammered into the final tie by a Japanese general. His repeated attempts failed and it was left to a prisoner to, appropriately, finish the job.

Very soon, Charles was on the move again and was surprised to find himself back at Nong Pladuk, on the junction of the Singapore-Bangkok main line, where the Burma-Siam railroad started.

1. Charles with his father and step-brother, Ken.

2. Exercises with the Kent Yeomanry on the South Downs, 1938.

3. ...and after the action; clean, clean, clean.

4. Charles and his BEF comrades in Northern France, 1939.

5. Watching a dogfight over Perenchies, 1940.

6. Charles has a hasty wash during retreat, Belgium, May 1940.

7. Dunkirk, 31 May 1940. Belgian and British soldiers waiting on the front to be evacuated.

8. A quiet moment on the beach. The rescuing ships are dimly seen.

9 HMS *Express*, which carried Charles safely back to England.

10. Charles and Louise reunited after Dunkirk.

11. Louise Crane in uniform, 1941.

12. *Top:* 135th (Herts. Yeomanry) Field Regiment RA, 336th Battery.

13. *Centre:* Exercises in Yorkshire during the summer of 1941. Charles is on the far right.

14. *Bottom:* The wedding photo which Charles carried throughout his captivity. Note Japanese censor's stamp.

15. MV *Sobieski.*

16. USS *Mount Vernon.*

17. Charles in Mombasa, Kenya, in December 1941.

18. Attap huts, Malaya.

19. Singapore river barges.

20. Certificate of Initiation presented to Charles on crossing the equator.

21. Singapore: the causeway across the Johore Strait.

No. Dw. 3/W. 30HO/87 9H00

(If replying, please quote above No.)

Army Form B. 104—83A.

...Record Office,

...Station.

...19

RA. RECORD & PAY OF.
FIELD BRANCH
—1 OCT 1943
FOOT'S CRAY, SIDCUP

SIR OR MADAM,

I have to inform you that a report has been received from the War Office to the effect that (No.) 87 9H00

(Rank) W/Sgt. (Name) STEEL. Charles Wilfred

(Regiment) Royal Artillery (Field)

is a Prisoner of War in Japanese Hands. Camp Unknown.

C.O. Japanese Red Cross, Tokyo.

Should any other information be received concerning him, such information will be at once communicated to you.

Instructions as to the method of communicating with Prisoners of War can be obtained at any Post Office.

I am,

SIR OR MADAM,

Your obedient Servant,

Officer in charge of Records.

IMPORTANT.—Any change of your address should be immediately notified to this Office. It should also be notified, if you receive information from the soldier above, that his address has been changed.

Wt.30241/1250 500M. 9/39. KJL/8818 Gp.698/3 Forms/B.104—83A/6

22. Official notification of Charles' capture.

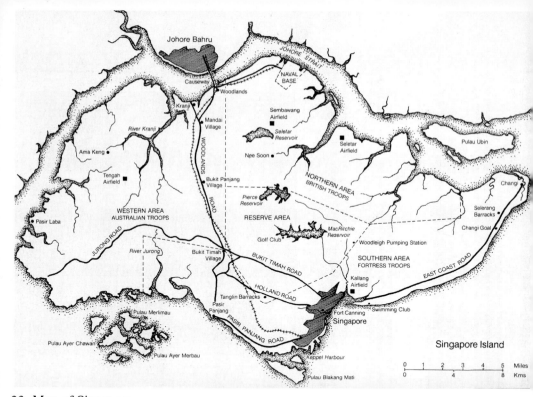

23. Map of Singapore.
24. Layout sketch of Tamarkan POW camp and location of the two railway bridges.

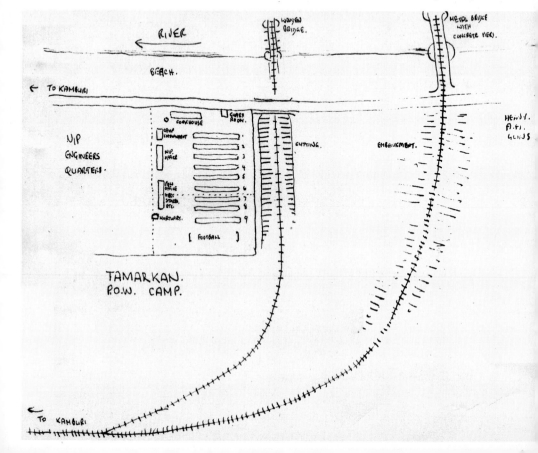

POW graves near Tamarkan, Thailand '43

River near No.7 POW camp, Thailand '43

Tamarkan – hills and camp '43

G. room – Tamarkan '43

Cookhouse by night – rice '43

Cookhouse by night – stew '43

25. Scenes from Tamarkan.

26. Sketches of two types of barges that Charles made in Letter 53. (See page 58.)

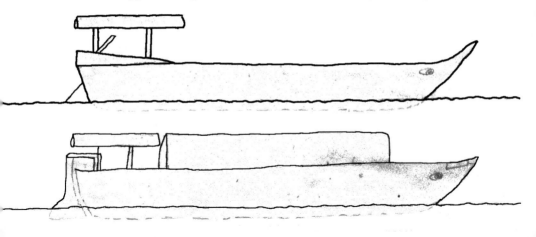

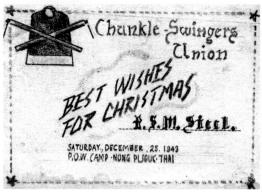

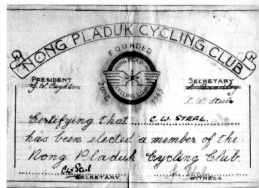

27. 'The Chunkle Swingers Union' Christmas card, Nong Pladuk, 25 December 1943.

28. Nong Pladuk Cycling Club membership certificate.

29. Drawings showing bridge piling.

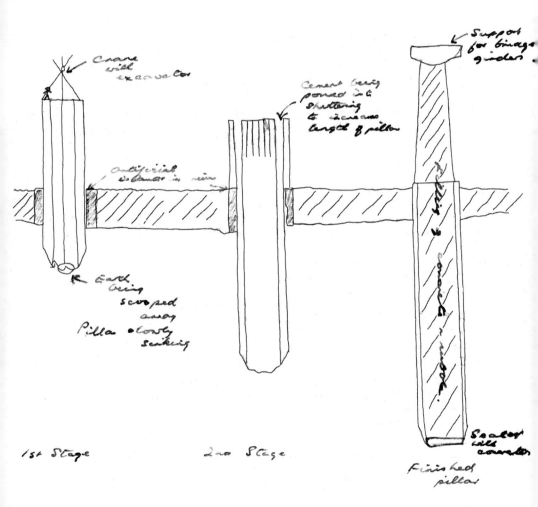

0. Completed railway, near Kinsiok.

1. One of the many trackside cemeteries.

he waited 3½ years for this to be dropped from the skies:– 28 Aug 1945.

TO ALL ALLIED PRISONERS OF WAR

THE JAPANESE FORCES HAVE SURRENDERED UNCONDITIONALLY AND THE WAR IS OVER

WE will get supplies to you as soon as it is humanly possible and we will make arrangements to get you out. Because of the distances involved it may be some time before we can achieve this.

YOU will help us and yourselves if you act as follows:

1. Stay in your camp until you get further orders from us.

2. Start preparing nominal rolls of personnel giving the fullest particulars.

3. List your most urgent necessities.

4. If you have been starved and underfed for long periods do not eat large quantities of solid food, fruit or vegetables at first. It is dangerous for you to do so. Small quantities at frequent intervals are much safer and will strengthen you far more quickly.

   For those who are really ill or very weak fluids such as broths and soups, making use of the water in which rice and other foods have been boiled, are much the best.

   Gifts of food from the local population should be cooked. We want to get you back home quickly, safe and sound, and we do not want you to risk getting diarrhoea, dysentery and cholera at this last stage.

5. Local authorities and/or Allied officers will take charge of your affairs in a very short time. Be guided by their advice.

32. Leaflet dropped by RAF announcing that the war was over.

33. Lord Louis Mountbatten in Singapore at the end of the war.

34. On the way home. *Left to right:* Sergeants Parsons and Edwards, with Charles Steel in Suez, Egypt.

35. WO2 Charles Steel, 1945.

36. Captain Louise Steel, 1945.

37. Prince's landing stage, Liverpool.

38. Charles visits the bridge, 1973.

39. Louise by the bridge, 1973.

Chapter 9

Return to Nong Pladuk

Letter 106 Nong Pladuk Aug'43
My Dearest,
   We were moved here on the 20th. Apparently we shouldn't have gone to Chungkai – the Nip army is like that.
   Nong Pladuk Camp was the first camp to be built in Thailand. It stands at the junction of the new Thailand – Burma line with the existing Bangkok – Singapore line. It is exactly 40 miles from Bangkok. It has as CO, Lt. Col. W.E. Gill, 137 Field Reg RA, and administration has been brought to a high level. Food is good, if monotonous, and there is a Chinese Canteen, a Dutch Canteen and a British Canteen, a Concert Party and a Church. At the moment I am officially sick but am anxious to start doing some work again as one must live and this needs money. Work here is at either Hashimoto's or Sakimolo's (Nip RAOC & RE units). At the moment I am in a mixed hut in charge of a section but expect to be soon transferred to the Gunner's Hut.

Nong Pladuk had been established for some fourteen months and the prisoners had been commanded by Lt.Col.Gill, who had gained respect in the same way as Col.Toosey had for standing up to the Japanese and, under the circumstances, for running a well ordered camp. The camp held about 2,000 men, mostly British and Dutch, but also some Australians and Americans.

Because of its important position as the junction between the two major rail links in Thailand, there was a complex of marshalling yards and engineering workshops. The prison cage itself was vulnerably sited within this obvious target for Allied bombers, as was soon, tragically, to be born out.

Nong Pladuk was to be Charles's home for the next eighteen months. The grimness of the previous months began to be replaced by routine and boredom, which can be detected in Charles's next few letters, as he casts around for something of interest to write about.

My Dear,

I wonder if a note on bananas would interest you? The banana tree is of the same fleshy substance as a hyacinth or daffodil. It grows up, bears leaves, has one crop of fruit and is then pulped for pig food. The leaves are a delicate green, are broad and readily split when blown by the wind. They are used instead of paper to wrap up purchases at markets everywhere in the east. The fibres of the stem are used for string and rope making.

The flowers are produced on a terrific stem, which comes out of the centre of the plant and the bud is about 9 inches long and a reddish colour. The bud opens and stamens can be seen under each set of petals. The petals then die away, leaving the tiny bananas. These rapidly swell until they are normal size. They should be picked green and kept under cover while ripening. Incidentally, there are plenty of straight bananas out here! I am going out in charge of the LS Party for light sick or squashi bioki, if you prefer it in Jap. I do no work after taking them to Hashimoto, but yesterday, while talking to a Nip, I discovered I was an artist.

I was telling him about up-country – and the elephants. Now Jap for elephant is ZOE, but he couldn't understand me so I drew something like a shaggy carthorse. Strange to say he recognised this and insisted that I should sit at his desk and draw elephants on his issue post cards for his kids.

In a few weeks I haven't any doubt that Little Muddleton on

the Slosh in Japland will be excited to receive these examples of British art. Hmm!

Nong Pladuk Sept'43
  You would laugh heartily if you could see to what lengths I have had to go to appear decently dressed. I am well off compared to most people, but nevertheless am forced to practice the most extensive economy in clothes. I have never flogged any clothing to the Thais and have still one good pair of KD shorts and one shirt that I am saving for freedom.
  Soon the patches will join up and I shall have a new pair of shorts!!

Letter 110
  A search today, but I lost nothing. These letters were safely hidden. Everyone is beginning to wear 'clip clops' – the native clog that can be bought or made cheaply. The difficulty is to learn how to keep them on one's feet. I have at last conquered this disinclination to 'stay on' and am now saving my boots on every possible occasion.

Letter 111
My Darlingest,
  You will be amazed to hear that a Cycling Club existed in a POW Camp in Thailand!! On arrival here, I was dumbfounded to find the 'NONG PLADUK CYCLING CLUB' holding weekly meetings, at which lectures are given and discussions take place. I have joined, of course. There are several CTC members, besides members of other clubs.

The Nong Pladuk Cycle Club was formed in June 1943 by G.W. Houghton and, for obvious reasons, never organized a single run. Its activities consisted of bi-weekly meetings at which lectures on racing, touring, cycle equipment and similar subjects were given. Quizzes on all subjects relating to cycling were very popular amongst the members, which included Australians, Dutch and cyclists from Great Britain. Towards the end of 1943, increasing Japanese pressure and strict orders against meetings of all sorts drove the club underground, but the meetings continued to take place at night in the darkness behind mosquito netting.

Letter 112 Nong Pladuk Oct'43

Darling,

I was sent for by Col.Gill yesterday, who said that the camp was allowed two MPs – an Officer and an OR. The OR had recently got into trouble with the Nips through selling goods to the Chinese (which he was supposed to stop) and a new MP had to be found. I had been recommended (who by?) and would I take the job. I wasn't particularly keen (all coppers are b . . . . . . s!) but he kept on, so finally was sent to Japs to be inspected and finally approved.

My duties are to stop men selling their kit to the Chinese and regulate the Chinese Canteen opening hours: also stop stealing if possible. For two men in a camp of 2,000 this is nearly impossible, but the general idea is to let the men sell to the Chinese, but to watch everything that goes through this – the only channel with the outside world. On the other hand, if the Nips catch me allowing the men to deal with the Chinese – well, I cop out. A complicated situation!!

Letter 113

The Chinese have attempted to bribe me with food, but I am not having any. We have been fairly successful in picking up some stolen goods by keeping a watch on stuff flogged. The RSM here is RSM Sandy MacTavish of the 2 Argyll's – a very good bloke indeed. I get on well with him.

The Secretary of the NCC (Nong Pladuk Cycling Club) has died and have become Hon. Sec. in his place. I gave a lecture on 'My First Tour' t'other evening. Some lectures are very good. We have Australian and Dutch cyclists as members besides British. Quizzes are very popular.

The Canteen is small, but makes pea soup out of tangy beans – this is rich in B1 and costs only 5c for 1/3 pint. Eggs are 10c.

Nov'43

I am out of work again. The IJA suddenly cut down the inside staff and have replaced me with another officer. Many Cookhouse people thrown out, too.

Never mind. The work is not hard and I am always in charge of the party anyway. The Camp band plays us out to work here and the other afternoon we were photographed. I have just come out of hospital after an attack of malaria. Better now, thanks.

After two years, which must have tested Charles's resolve, he received his first letter from Louise a moment he noted with a rare dated response.

Letter 115 Nong Pladuk 8.11.43
My Dearest Darling,

This is one of the big moments of my life. Today I came in from work to find some mail waiting for me. One letter from you, one from Shirley, 2 from Bow.

I read your's first, then gave the men's out to my section. Oh my dear, I cannot put my feelings on paper. I have become uplifted. I cannot eat. I simply laid down on my blanket and trembled like a leaf. Laugh if you will, but that's the effect your letter had on me. To know you are well and alive last September '42. Oh my darling, how could I doubt you when I had no news in the first lot of mail? This one letter has made all the difference. One day I shall return to you. Nothing will stop me. I will myself to live for that day. I love you dearly, Louie sweetheart.

A little while later, he continued.

My Dear,

Being a little calmer, I must thank you for my first letter for over two years. You don't know what it means to me. I wish you could have written in more detail but undoubtedly the censors would have objected. I wonder where your Course took place?

Honestly, darling, I do feel an awful 'Has been' when I read your letter. Nevertheless, I love you deeply.

December at Nong Pladuk brought another change for Charles. Once again he found himself involved with the administration of the all-important camp canteen, something that was to prove a turning point of his captivity. It also coincided with the reappearance of his old commanding officer, Colonel Toosey, who arrived from Tamakan on 11 December, and was instrumental in appointing Charles to his Staff.

> *Letter 119 Nong Pladuk Dec'43*
> *I am on the Staff again!*
> *A few days ago there was a big scandal in the Canteen. A Bdr employed for making soup was caught making more soup than he was ordered, selling the surplus and pocketing the money. I'm ordered to prevent this sort of thing, I have been asked by the PRI (Major Featherstone) to become manager of the PRI, with all the varied branches. The PRI Canteen has to be able to swallow up the many thousands of dollars paid by the IJA to the men every 10 days.*
> *At the moment I am learning the ropes on the Cooked Foods side. The PRI is Major Featherstone (Baluches). The Canteen officer is Lt. Fullerton (RA) and the officer i/c cooked foods is Lt. Cowie (FAISUR).*

The IJA had taken over the prisoners' canteens in September and put a stop to all profits being made. These small profits had enabled the hospitals to purchase medicines on the black-market, but with this source of revenue closed, another method of fund-raising had to be implemented.

With Charles managing the canteen, he had become party to a scheme that channelled thousands of dollars away from the Japanese and into a secret fund that financed drugs and medicines for the sick. This involved what is now euphemistically described as 'creative accounting' and took the form of two sets

94

of accounts; one for the Japanese and the prisoner's own true ledger. As this eventually involved thousands of dollars kept from the Japanese, Charles refrained from mentioning this in his letters until he was liberated.

Meanwhile, another all male Christmas was celebrated.

Letter 120 Nong Pladuk Christmas '43
My Dear,

We had an Air Raid warning today!! A fine time to know that our boys are about!!

At the same time we shall begin to dig trenches!!

Christmas once again, away from the world. How many more . . . ?

At the Canteen we have cooked over 120 Christmas puddings – mostly rice, I'm afraid, but successfully disguised with plenty of limes and cloves and bananas. 10c a slice with sauce. We have worked hard all day today and I haven't had time to see the pantomime, 'Cinderella'.

We have some fine 'women' for the finale leads. In the evening, we had a combined units RA Christmas Dinner in the Gunners tent amongst all RA WOs and Sjts. We invited Col. Toosey, who has been transferred from Tamarkan, Col. Gill (137), the Camp Padre and the MO. I made the toast to 'The Guests'. The food was quite good and included some 'wine' made from fermented rice. It was suprising how many different RA units were present; AA, Anti-Tank, Field, Coast, all kinds.

Here's to Christmas next year with my darling. God Bless Her!!

Herewith, the recipe for POW's Xmas Pudding, if you are interested in ERSATZ productions. 400 portions

> *32 gallons cooked rice*
> *12.5 kgs potatoes*
> *48 limes*
> *1.5 kgs green ginger*
> *4.5 kgs pork fat*

200 bananas
18 kgs rice flour
6 coconuts
18 kgs brown sugar
cloves etc.

The Nong Pladuk Camp was gradually enlarged until it housed about 8,000 prisoners. A small hospital was built and sports were allowed. Overall, conditions were gradually improved and vastly better than the jungle camps that most of the men had endured. Rations were still monotonous and the Red Cross comforts were systematically plundered by the guards. It was not only the Red Cross supplies that were not reaching the prisoners but it was common knowledge that the Japanese and Korean NCOs ran rackets which involved the pilfering of the prisoners' rations resulting in great reduction in their food.

> *There are rumours that a hospital is to be built at Nakom Paton to house the sick of all groups. All POWs are organised into 6 main groups (2 in Burma and 4 in Thailand). This will be a good thing if the Nips give medicines, drugs etc to keep it going. Knowing the Nips, this doesn't seem to ring true.*

Charles seems to have suffered a depression after the euphoria he experienced after Louise's letter. In fact, during January, he wrote only one short note.

> *January 8 '43*
> *My Dear,*
> *What a delightful New Year gift!! My second lot of mail – but how disappointed I was when I missed your handwriting! Some from Bow, some from Shirley and one from the Aunt in Yorkshire, but none from the person I _really_ want to hear from. I do hope nothing is wrong.*
> *We also had some so-called Red Cross comforts: ½ tablet Chinese soap and 19 unsmokeable native cigarettes. What a farce it is! I do hope you are not being pestered (by the Red*

Cross) for something at home. One might as well make a donation to the Jap Army Corps.

A desperate Charles Steel wrote in February;

A few men have been allowed to send full length letters home. These were decided upon by ballot. I 'bought' two lines in a letter written by a Gnr.Butler, in which he asks his wife to get in touch with you. I wonder if they will ever get home?

His 'black' mood continued with news of another atrocity.

The full story of the murder of two British Officers by the Japs at Kanburi (sic) has just come out. The Japs found a radio that was made of odds and sods and promptly beat up the officers concerned until they were dead!! Nice people in charge of us!!

The discovery of a hidden radio, which received the nightly news from Delhi, resulted in the killing of Captain Hawley RASC and the severe beating of Major Slater RA. After the war, the Japanese major responsible for this crime and the general ill-treatment of POWs was found guilty and executed.

Letter 126
A few notes from this Camp.
A few items of sports gear received from YMCA. Nips take up sports.
Many inspections by 'high Japanese Officers' – usually Majors. An officer and OR sent to Singapore and Bangkok to broadcast.
Spate of lectures. We are running lectures in the Canteen after closing hours. Lectures almost every night. I gave one, 'Eight months in France'.
Col.Toosey cleaning up camp rapidly.
PRI changed. Now Major Marsh (RAOC)
Apple Dutch-type cake very popular at Canteen.

97

Meat pies 10c gaining in popularity. Enormous quantities of pea soup sold.

Concert party excelling itself with productions. 'Hi Gang', 'When Day is Over', 'Eosapado Argentina'. I usually get a seat in the wings.

Radio broadcasters return. Interesting lectures about conditions in Malaysia.

HURRAY – letter from Louie – it's worth its weight in gold!!

With the receipt of Louie's letter, Charles's mood became more upbeat. He did report, however, an incident that later had unpleasent repercussions.

Letter 128 Nong Pladuk April '44
My Dearest,

We have just moved from Hut 5 to a new bamboo and attap hut at the back of the Camp. I could live in the Canteen if I wished, but prefer to have somewhere to retire to. One gets no rest in the Canteen.

Incidentally, I have just had a rather exciting night. Eggs and soap have been missing from the Canteen, so I stopped up all night and at about 5–30am caught the Australian cooks who are on the staff, helping themselves. They left that day!! It was quite exciting in the dark.

In stopping the Australians' little racket, Charles had made a couple of enemies who sought immediate revenge, so forever souring Charles's opinion of Australians.

Letter 163

On two consecutive nights following the one on which I caught the Australians stealing from the Canteen (at Nong Pladuk), I found scorpions in my bed. On one occasion I didn't find it until morning. Nevertheless, I was not stung.

Charles then waxes lyrical on the attributes of bamboo, the mango and the virtues of mosquito nets.

Bamboo is the most remarkable wood in the world. Anyway, it really is a giant grass. It is circular and consists of hollow sections. It is very strong and sharp, if broken. From bamboo, one can make cups, pots, scoops, brooms, pencil holders, pens. One can build the complete framework of a building, make the roof of split bamboo and move in within a few days. One only needs string or ties to hold the bamboo together. One can split the inside and use the white inner surface for writing upon.

A Dutchman in the camp is now making single and double water pumps out of bamboo and odd pieces of shoe leather. They work well.

The Japs use big male bamboo for water pipes and chimneys. They use the small thin ones for beating up purposes!!

The mango – the grandest of the many tropical fruits to my mind.

The mango is of a peculiar shape and has a large stone. In good varieties mangoes, the stone, although as long as the fruit, is very, very narrow and there is, consequently, plenty of luscious meaty fruit on both sides. The flavour of the mango is between that of a peach and an orange.

IT IS DELICIOUS . . . but some people , who have lived in the East for many years, say that it causes skin diseases. Strangely enough, the scent of the mango is irresistible to flies.

Dysentery is certain. Buy them green and let them ripen under cover from flies. For some years now, I have slept under a mosquito net – a thing one doesn't think of in England. I am fortunate in saving mine at the Capitulation – people who haven't got them are suffering terribly from malaria.

There are many kinds.

British Army IP type.

Japanese and Dutch type.

British Officers type.

If one is resident in a place like Malaya, one has a wire cage installed in one's bedroom, so one can sleep without a net close to one's person. They are inclined to be hot.

I'd love to be inside a net with you . . .

Charles had definitely recovered from his bout of depression!

> *Letter 133 Nong Pladuk May'44*
> *Some notes:-*
> *Parties still going up jungle – whenever possible, people who haven't been before. Great new theatre built. Permission given by one Japanese Sjt. Permission refused by t'other. Great argument between the two. A great failing of the IJA; no two departments ever work together.*
> *Rumours of a landing in France.*
> *Chinese Canteen closed to POWs. We like our noodles and other Chinese dishes. Some USA Red Cross received. One individual parcel given to over 10 men. Nips living like lords. I do wish the Red Cross could see what is happening and stop sending this stuff to the Nips.*
> *Red Cross goods bought with British Govt. money through the Swiss Consul arrived – ½ bar soap and 1 biscuit per man!*
>
> *June 1944*
> *Invasion of France seems successful and has put great heart into us. Wish we were there! Sick being sent out to work. One man (Dutch) collapsed and died.*
> *A large party left the Camp en route for Japan via Singapore*

With the railway completed and supply trains running up to Burma, the Japanese looked to use their captives on other labour-intensive projects like factories, mines and airfield construction. Charles was lucky to remain in the relatively comfortable Nong Pladuk Camp, at least for the time being.

> *I am very fortunate in having held the job for 6 months. It has resulted in my being very fit, although I am officially sick with eye trouble to prevent the Japanese claiming me for outside work.*
> *The Canteen is very big now and turns over money at the rate of half-a million a year! Almost 100 employees. Anything from a cigarette to a meal – cakes, toffees, meat, pies, fruit – every-*

thing that human originality can devise. I have had my pay put up and am living comfortably. This is a very good experience. There are a number of Dutch on the staff who specialise in sambals and Javanese dishes. I should like to show you round as I have done to so many Jap officers.

August 1944
My Dearest,

Further parties of men are leaving for Japan. I wonder when I shall go? If I do, I'm afraid that I shall lose these letters because the search is a very thorough one indeed and papers are all destroyed. Conditions in Singapore are reported to be appallingly bad with regard to food. Housing is OK, of course. The idea is, I believe, to put us to work in factories. To this end, everyone had had to put down one's trade. (This must have perplexed the Japanese to find that the British were a nation of hairdressers.) We have also been tested for cholera (glass tube method – I must tell you some laughable incidents here). Some day . . .

The 137 Field Regt RA is strongly represented in this Camp. It hails from Blackpool and has many of its original TA members in it. It came out here on 'Dominion Monarch' just before the Nip war began and it was in action the whole way down Malaya. It lost heavily at Slim River, which was one of the bad patches of the campaign.

The men in the 137 are a good crowd and mix well with those of the 135. I get on fairly well with Lancashire people and have made many friends and acquaintances.

Bowing to pressure from his canteen commander, Charles agreed to move into the canteen to keep a twenty-four hour watch on what had grown into a money spinning enterprise, the significance of which he could not reveal in writing for fear of discovery.

I have at last capitulated and have moved to the Canteen, where I am sleeping in the toffee factory!!

Whenever August comes around, I always remember with great happiness our last leave but one in August '41. I enjoyed that leave more than our last because it was the last we had together all the time. The weather was delightful – do you remember picking the apples in the orchard? And I, for one, was really happy. Thank goodness we took plenty of photographs to keep those memories forever!

Chapter 10

Bombed by the RAF

The routine of camp life, which had Charles struggling to write about anything interesting, was suddenly shattered, not by the Japanese, but by the Royal Air Force. With the Allies gaining control of the air, it was inevitable that the railway would become a target. Unfortunately, in targeting a depot like Nong Pladuk, the RAF seemed unaware that the POW camp was situated in its centre and resultant carnage caused great resentment.

Letter 140 Nong Pladuk 7 September 1944
My Darling,
 This is terrible . . .
 We have had Allied aircraft flying overhead on numerous occasions. Sometimes the Free Indian AA opens up with their Bofors from their nearby camp. This morning at 2 am, I was awakened by the Indians firing and the steady drone of aircraft overhead. And then the bombs came shrieking down. I was petrified in my half-awake condition. Fortunately I was only about 6 inches off the ground. Bombs seemed to explode all around the Camp. Splinters whistled through the flimsy bamboo and attap of the huts. One chunk passed directly over me. I rolled out of bed and laid on the ground before the next stick fell.
 I then went over to the Gunners' hut to see if anyone was hurt. Here there were only minor injuries. The RAF then turned

their attention to our oil dump near by and great fires were soon blazing.

As soon as it was possible to move about, we found that four bombs had been placed directly across the centre of our Camp, while another stick had fallen down one side. The scenes were gruesome in the extreme as the bombs had exploded while the POWs were lying asleep, tightly packed in the huts.

At the moment I am waiting to take part in a mass burial. All day, the victims have been dying, until now there must be 80 or 90 laid out on the blood soaked ground on hastily made stretchers. The IJA refused to allow a light during the night for emergency operations. No Jap was injured. The Nip Sgt, on seeing the rows of seriously injured said 'OK-speedo finish'. They think it is very funny for our own planes to bomb us.

We don't: this camp has been here for 3 years now – is our intelligence service so bad as to think that this is a Nip camp? We are feeling rather bitter towards the RAF today.

The prisoners had suffered over 400 casualties including over ninety killed or who died of wounds. As Charles noted, there were no Japanese casualties. The fates certainly seemed to conspire against the weak and helpless. Frustration and resentment threatened to boil over and the Japanese were quick to allow the prisoners to dig slit trenches but would not resite the camp away from the railway. They did, however, take the precaution of moving their own accommodation a safe distance from the railway.

Letter 141
The funeral was the most appalling ceremony ever. The Nips promised transport – then altered their mind when it was growing dark. About 350 men then picked up the bodies on the rice sack stretchers to carry them to the cemetery – a mile away. This was the signal for a tremendous rainstorm, which caused the stretchers to come to pieces and caused the bearers great difficulty in carrying the bodies, which slipped out.

Overall was the realisation that if the RAF came back that night, many more would be in the same position the following night. It was ghastly. The Thais fled at our approach. The stench of the broken bodies appalling.

Trenches have been hastily dug in the Camp and a system of alarms instituted. The whole camp was out in the trenches during the night because a diesel train passed along the railway. Everyone's nerves are raw because the Japs have threatened to shoot anyone who breaks out of the Camp to reach safety. It's an awful feeling to be cooped up in a small area with the knowledge that the RAF think we are Nips.

The Japs will not allow us to mark the Camp with the Red Cross. Darling, if we ever meet again, I'm going to tie myself securely to your apron strings . . .

The consequences of the bombing continued to dominate the prisoners.

Letter 142
My Dear,

Sjt. Norris (344 Bty) died today. He was in the Hospital, which suffered very severely indeed from the bombing. There is a rumour that the BBC have broadcast a report on the successful bombing of a Nip Transit Camp . . . Casualties are now nearly 100 dead, very many badly damaged with legs off, etc. It is an awful thing.

We are spending a lot of time up now at night but hope that when the moon goes down we shall get some sleep.

Col. Toosey has written to the Nip Officer commanding all POWs, asking for the camp to be marked and the British Govt. notified that we are here.

Letter 143 Nong Pladuk October 1944

The next Camp to us (Nong Pladuk II) has been amalgamated with this one and IJA staff from there have taken over here. I am being retained here.

The Canteen is now very large, with a cigarette factory, quick lunch bar, supper bar and a whole host of amenities.

The Dutch had established the 'Fag Fabrik', which produced rough hand-rolled cigarettes of coarse native tobacco wrapped in rice paper. These were variously named 'Sikh's Beard' or 'Hag's Bush' and were a great inducement to kick the habit.

The Officers, with their 50 dollars a month are the chief customers, although men who steal from the IJA on working parties and sell to the Thais, have a lot of money – and they spend it.

These notes are now being buried deep down, in view of the incriminating words.

Letter 144 November 1944

The Accounts of the canteen now have to be kept in Japanese fashion, which is rather amusing because even the IJA can't understand them.

A Jap Colonel has arrived from Japan to take over all groups of POWs. Reported to have beaten up a Jap Major at a bad camp up country.

Supplies of Canteen changed by Nips from Chinese to Thai. Lorry arrives every morning with a cute little Thai girl in charge. About 21, not more than 4'6" tall, perfectly proportioned – gives us all naughty thoughts, but an armed Korean guard with her . . . She obviously knows she is IT! But does she know she is raped – in imagination by about 3,000 men per day?

A lot of staff cutting. Parties still going up country, sick coming down. I seem permanent. More mail arrived – thank you, darling – more than I can ever say.

The routine was again broken by another RAF bombing raid which, although it only caused minor casualties, frayed the nerves of men already close to breaking point.

Letter 145 November 1944
My Darling,

They've done it again!!

We were in the trenches all last night and although no bombs

fell in the Camp, the RAF missed the railway line and the bombs
fell on the roadway by the Cookhouse, which was partly blown
down and set on fire. Only a few minor injuries this time, thank
goodness.

I looked up once and saw a huge 4-engine bomber pass across
the face of the moon – straight over the Camp. The black silhou-
ette seemed to represent all that was evil in the world – and yet
– they are our own planes, with our own flesh and blood –
perhaps Ken himself –inside them. This is a ghastly mix up. The
Dutch are inclined to panic. It takes a lot to keep still.

Charles's younger stepbrother, Ken, volunteered for the RAF
with the expressed intention of liberating his beloved sibling. He
was not, however, involved in the bombing raids on the railway.

There was also a tightening of security by the Japanese, not
to prevent escaping, but rather to restrict nocturnal black-
market trading. This just added to the tension and frustration
felt by men about to enter their third year in captivity.

Letter 146 Nong Pladuk November 1944
My Dear,
The IJA have ordered that all valuables have to be handed in.
I am one of the few with a watch left – but have hidden this
below ground and handed in a cheap broken one which I
bought for a few dollars. Pencil and pen are also below ground.
I shall be shot if these notes are ever found as no diaries are
allowed; besides, the possession of pens and pencils is
forbidden, I hate giving in to these bastards on any point. We
are not likely to see these valuables back if I know the IJA. As
I can't use mine any more, I think that I shall sell it by 'under-
ground' methods and possibly change the proceeds into a
sterling cheque through a 'hard-up' officer.

Restrictions are becoming very severe. At last the IJA have
got a POW administration working – and mighty uncomfort-
able it is, too! Each hut commander must report every two
hours during the day where all his men are! And during the
night, each hut must have two guards on duty (sin bars) to stop

men escaping! Every hour, a Korean guard comes round and attempts to count the bodies lying in rows. He usually gets muddled up and finds a man in the latrine whom the 'sin bars' didn't know was out and then it's slap, slap, bash, bang for the bloke on duty.

These Koreans ought to be punished severely for these crimes. The gunzo here now is named Takashima. He is inordinately vain and is known as Handsome Charlie. He is an expert at pinpricking. He is quiet and never bashes anyone himself but is the most infuriating man I have ever met. He will cancel a concert ten minutes before it begins or suddenly announce that there must be no _talking_ on the stage, no _laughter_ among the audience. Or he will stop a football match if he sees the Koreans enjoying it. Or, perhaps, send half our staff out to work without notice. I'd like to kill him!

We have a Major Chida, the No.1 Group Commander in the Camp now. He is known as 'Dad' or the 'DOC' (that's naughty, I admit). He is very ancient, almost bent double and puts one in mind of an old chicken. He gets drunk regularly and, in spite of his senility, is a lad with the girls who attend him regularly. He is not seen for a day or so after a visit from one of the Comfort girls, who come from Ban Pong to minister to his needs. He is terribly absent minded. One day he fell down a disused latrine.

Charles's hopes of making a profit from selling his watch were soon dashed.

It looks as if I have dropped the proverbial clanger. I sent my watch out by a man who contacts Thais and now the working party on which the man goes is now cancelled owing to cholera at that particular Japanese Camp. It looks as if I have lost my watch . . . PS. It won't worry me as long as I get back to you. The Japs can have all my belongings, the Government can have all my credits. I shall be content to get back in my birthday suit . . . I'm sure you won't mind!

Charles launched into one of his frequent declarations of love, which the lengthy separation had not diminished.

My Dear,
   I sometimes think we shall be here twenty years and get correspondingly downhearted. But however long it is, Louie, nothing is going to be altered as far as you and I are concerned, This poem rather fitted with my mood.

   Let Her grow lovely, growing old,
   So many fine things to do,
   Laces and ivories and gold
   And silks need not be new.

   There is beauty in old trees,
   Old streets a glamour hold;
   Why may not She, as well as these,
   Grow lovely, growing old?

   So even if we are in our seventies when we meet again, darling, you will still be 21 in my eyes!!

Charles and his comrades had to endure yet another Christmas in captivity.

Nong Pladuk Christmas 1944
My Dear,
   Another Christmas apart!! When _is_ this going to end? Looking back, it seems amazing that we could live on hope in 1942. And yet now, almost into 1945, we still hope from day to day. I am even still shaving daily, so you see that I haven't become a savage entirely yet.
   The IJA have given everyone a tiny portion of saki (which we have paid for out of Canteen profits). They are extraordinary people. They have now moved from their Administrative building, which is near the railway and put POWs in there to sleep. Every time an engine starts up in the night, the whole hut flies out of the doors and windows and into the trenches. Some have taken up the floorboards to facilitate hurried exits.

The Cookhouse is now moved to a safer quarter. I hear the new Canteen is to be built further away from the railway.

I wonder what you are doing today? My thoughts are with you. However long this enforced parting is going to be, we're going to be back together some day.

If Christmas at Nong Pladuk was dull, the RAF made certain that New Year got off to a bang.

Nong Pladuk 31 December 1944
My Dear,

Once again the RAF has paid us an unwelcome visit. I was just finishing my tea, when I heard the bugle and heard men running. I went out to the trench and saw a sight which froze my blood.

Approaching from the East, in perfect formation, in broad daylight and at not more than 5,000 feet were 12 four engined bombers. The AA opened up and I dived. Then came the bombs. Although apparently overhead, most of the bombs fell on Hashimoto's railway yard and only a few fell on the camp. One lump of red hot metal fell between me and Mr. Fullerton. After they had passed, came second and third waves; the first two dumped high explosives, the third incendiaries. The Dutch panicked after the first wave.

There was indescribable damage at Hashimoto's. In the Camp, too. Major Sykes and another officer were killed besides several men. The Hospital was burnt completely down. Two other huts were almost destroyed. The Cookhouse was completely destroyed. Men are walking about with just a ball bag on, having lost all other kit. Many men with mental disorders. The strain of being Aunt Sallies is rather great.

I was to have a further thrill.

The Cookhouse was burnt down but we had a lot of four gallon tins on a range there. As we took over the job of brewing tea for all the Camp until a new Cookhouse was established, I went down with my coffee man – Sjt Mayes – at about 3am to look for any undamaged cans. Vain hope! We returned

unlucky. No sooner had we returned to the Canteen, when a
tremendous explosion shook the Camp. A delayed action bomb
under the Cookhouse had blown the debris to smithereens.

A lucky escape, for we must have been standing on it!!
Somehow I feel sure that I am ordained to come back to you . . .

It seemed incomprehensible to the POWs that British
Intelligence had not found out that the RAF were frequently
dropping bombs on their own men. Instead, the raids continued
on Nong Pladuk, with the odd stray bombs continuing to cause
casualties and distress in the Camp.

January 15 1945
My Dear,
   We have moved today to a big new Canteen built at the back
of the Camp. Things should be safer here, although a higher
water table doesn't allow such deep trenches. We are still
visiting these on moonlight nights and often during the day. The
RAF are very heavy handed.
   There are rumours that all the officers are being taken away
from us.

For Charles, the most significant anniversary was upon him
again, and again he had not yet celebrated it with his wife. He
expresses a nagging worry that affected most married prisoners
– would their relationship have changed by the enforced lengthy
parting? Sadly, for many, the long anticipated reunion would
soon turn to dust. Many released POWs were badly scarred by
their experiences at the hands of the Japanese and their wives
and families, who had also suffered great anxiety, were unable
to offer the sort of succour needed.

18 January 1945
My Darling,
   Once again <u>THE</u> day has come round. It is my ambition that
next year we shall be together on our most important day in the
year, I wonder?

On this day this year, I can reiterate the vows I made to you four years ago. Four years ago and not more than three weeks together!! I feel that it is almost criminal on my part to have married you and then left you tied up like this. My deepest hope is that when I get home, you will tell me everything is the same between us, that our companionship is worth waiting for, that you still love me with the same devotion that caused you to accept me in 1940. On my side, I can tell you that your personality and influence have saved my reason, that the fact that we are partners has given me the strongest possible impulse to live – because it wasn't the food that kept one alive in 1943.

As Charles intimated, the Japanese decided to separate the British officers from their men. In a repeat of the earlier exercise in 1942, when all senior officers had been segregated, the Japanese sought to upset the cohesion of the camp by removing all the officers and concentrating them at Kanchanaburi.

24 January 1945
My Dearest,
   A sad day in our lives as POWs as all the officers have been taken from us and sent to Kamburie (sic)
   RSM MacTavish (Argyll & Sutherlands) has taken over as Camp Commander from Col. Toosey, CSM Stadden (RASC) has taken over as Adjutant from Major Davidson, Staff Sergeant Shenning has taken over messing from Capt. Boyle, while I have taken on the job of PRI from Major Marsh, the Canteen from Lt. Fullerton and the 'underhand' work of the Finance Committee from Capt. Northcote, Lt. Fallerton and Lt. Neivede.
   A big portion on my plate – besides which, I happen to be the senior 135 OR here, so I have about 100 Gunners to cast an eye upon, too.
   The Colonel almost made me howl when he said 'au revoir'. He is a grand man! We no longer have officers to act as 'buffers' between ourselves and the Japanese.
   The WO's have got to toe the line, now.

The Nip officer, with whom I have to deal, is Lt. Oda, his Sjt. Major and the Koreans on Q Staff.

February '45

Things are going fairly well. I have introduced three new lines at the Canteen – lime Marmalade, rice rafts (for fried eggs) and fruit pies (which taste like apple pies).

In my dealings with the Nips, things have, so far, gone smoothly. At first, I used an interpreter but now find that Lt. Oda can speak bits of English and we get on fairly well. He isn't a bad cove, but the RSM is a bit of a turd. A lot of barking, but no bite so far. One of the Japanese 10 daily account forms is about five feet long by two feet wide. One walks round it to fill it in! There are so many regulations that one has to be very careful.

I have a very good clerk, L/BC1 Wright (137), who is a National Provincial Bank clerk. Most of my staff are gunners. RA people seem to do what they are told better than other units. I am paying two rates, 30c per day for executive job (disregarding rank) and 25c for general labour. I get 40c, together with the Dutch Ensign, who looks after the Dutch staff.

The regular bombing of Nong Pladuk and the rest of the railway, finally persuaded the Japanese to move their prisoners. This was not for humanitarian reasons but cold reality. The railway had not been a success, even when trains were able to travel unmolested along its length. At no stage did it carry the planned tonnage and was unable to deliver the supplies to sustain the IJA in Burma. With Japan clearly losing the war and with the Allies moving ever closer to the motherland, the prisoners were being hastily sent to work on projects aimed at defending the steadily deflating Greater Eastern Co-Prosperity Sphere, which was still acting as a buffer zone.

Letter 155 Nong Pladuk February '45

My Dearest,

We are moving. I have been instructed to shut down the Canteen by the middle of the month and have to hand the Canteen capital to the Nips for conveyance to the new camp. We are not allowed more than 20 dollars each.

Charles cryptically continues;

A lot of problems arise which I cannot mention here in case these notes get found. We are allowed to have just about nothing now, so anything we have has to be hidden securely – not easy in a move.

Where are we going? Most popular rumours say Indo-China, China or Korea. I wonder. Travelling as POW is the most awful experience ever; but they move their troops in the same way.

Chapter 11

Ubon

With Colonel Toosey and the rest of the officers now at Kachanaburi, sixty miles north of Nong Pladuk, Charles and the rest of the ORs found themselves transported over 300 miles away to the east, to the Thai-Indo China border. During the long journey, Charles and his companions passed through the Thai capital, Bangkok. They were struck not just by the beauty of the city but also the extensive bomb damage wreaked by the Allies, who now had complete mastery of the air. This was the first intimation that the tide of war could be turning against their captors.

Letter 156 Bangkok February '45
My Dearest,

We left Nong Pladuk on the 21ˢᵗ in the last party. We travelled by train towards Bangkok and saw the famous pagoda or temple or wat at Nakhon Pathom (City of Origin), which is a holy town, and finally got to a place called Nakhon Chase as it was getting dark. The railway ended here owing to the attentions of the RAF all night. We were kept crammed in the trucks and were eaten alive by mosquitoes.

The next morning, we started marching and found ourselves approaching a mighty river, which had once been spanned by a great steel bridge, which now reposed gracefully in the water, blown apart and twisted by the RAF.

The Nips had slung a wire and bamboo footbridge across the ruins of the bridge and, across this swaying, flimsy structure, we had to make our way. I was very pleased to get across.

On the other side, we waited hours until a train arrived with Burma-bound Nips. We got a shock here – 64 had to go on each truck. In every truck, about 20 had to climb up and travel on the roof.

We got to Bangkok – Venice of the East and City of Temples – about midday and were transferred into barges, which floated on the Menam, the great river, which is the artery of Thailand.

I had charge of a barge with 40 men, but suddenly noticed water creeping up the inside. After about an hour's argument with a Nip, I finally managed to get all but 10 shifted. I shall always remember the journey through Bangkok. The sun caught the gilded pagoda and the coloured tiles on the wats and threw glorious colours to us who, for so long, had seen nothing beautiful, clean or decent. It was amazing to see people wearing proper clothes again. In the garden of one house, we saw the French flag waving. Best of all, we saw some of our own internees (civilians).

We passed right through the City, down through the coconut plantations towards the sea. Where are we going?

The question was soon answered. A great row of warehouses ('go-downs') suddenly appeared on one side of the river. Surely they weren't going to put us in there – such an obvious target for the RAF.

Oh yes, they were! Into the 'go-downs' we went – and now we are packed like sardines on the concrete floor of the great warehouses – not allowed an exercise or movement outside the buildings.

Charles and his comrades were then transported 250 miles to the east to Ubon Ratchatani, close to the border with modern day Laos.

Letter 157 Ubon, Thailand March'45

My Dearest Girl,

We have arrived. We left the 'go downs' by trains in trucks (44 to each truck), which had recently carried oil and tar. It took until midday to get to Bangkok Station from the docks – about 4 kilos. We then waited outside the station. At about 2am, the air raid sirens blew. What a place to be in! The Nips hurriedly took us away from the railway and we laid on a lawn in front of a school until the all clear went.

The train left at 4am, drawn by a powerful Beyer-Garratt articulated locomotive. The damage done by the bombing was terrific. All that night, we travelled on and on eastward and all the next day. In the afternoon, we crossed a high range of mountains and descended again at Koret.

At about 6am the next morning we arrived at the railhead of Ubon in Eastern Thailand. To the south is Cambodia in Indo-China. We then crossed a great river (the Mekong) in sampans and marched north for nine kilos. There is no camp here what-soever. We are living in the open in paddy fields. I pray we shall have cover by the time the rains come, as all this area will be flooded.

I have already started up the Canteen on borrowed capital and today was successful in getting a little shelter, which is the acorn from which a thriving canteen is going to be built. You may laugh at the insistence and seriousness with which I mention a mere canteen, but one day I will be able to tell you the whys and wherefores.

I was successful today in persuading Lt. Oda to take me to Ubon with him. I doubted his word when he said he couldn't get fruit for me. He was right – this area is entirely rice growing and fruit is beyond our pockets. A grave question. Eggs are 20c too! I bought a pig t'other day and got choked off for it today.

Lt. Oda told me that all supplies would come through the IJA here, as 'there are no good merchants in this country'. This means high prices and plenty of rake-offs by Koreans.

Notes from Ubon

No fence around us yet.

Tobacco here in baskets and not in limpange.
A big camp is being built nearby by ourselves, for ourselves.
Main working parties on Sensitai Aerodrome, near Ubon.
Secondary working parties on Settitan Aerodrome near here.
One man caught in Ubon – an Australian named Merritt.
Nips took him out next day to show them where he went. Came
back and said he had been shot trying to escape. We were
allowed to get his body back. Obviously purposely done.
    Apparently a lot of mangos in this area in a month's time.
Have sent a typewritten post card home (25 words).

As the Allies increase their pressure on all fronts, so the Japanese began another crackdown on their captives.

Ubon April 1945
My Beloved,
    We are now in the yet-to-be-completed camp and the
Canteen is in the end bay of the Cookhouse. We work very
closely together. No more trips to Ubon. Restrictions are now
very tight. Plenty of nit-picking, the worst being the order to
crop our hair. You wouldn't recognise me, I'm sure. Men are
very badly off for clothes now – many almost naked.

The novelty of moving to a different area soon wore off and the mind-numbing monotony of captivity is reflected in the next letters, which concentrate on the natural world.

The scavenger of the East is the Turkey Buzzard – a kind of
vulture, which eats rubbish and especially dead dogs, cats,
offal etc.
    A large number are attracted to the Camp by the intestines
of the pigs, which are issued by the Japanese and which are
killed by us. The intestines are thrown to them and a terrible
fight ensues. Within seconds, everything is gobbled up and the
vultures fly slowly up to a tree to roost, or mount even higher
until they are circling specks in the sky.
    There are two remarkable insects around here.

The Stick Insect which is coloured like a dead stick and grows up to 6 inches long. Only if it falls to the ground or moves can one tell that it is alive.

Two more well known – if unpleasant-insects in Thailand.

The Centipede is poisonous, but not fatal. I was bitten by one the other day. My arm got fat and I felt as if I had malaria. They are olive green and very unpleasant customers.

Worse still are the scorpions. Again, the normal scorpion here is dangerous but not fatal. It attacks with the pincers and stings with a poisoned dart on the tail.

Charles then recalled the incident when he caught the two Australian cooks stealing from the Canteen at Nong Pladuk the previous April. They sought revenge by putting scorpions in Charles's bed.

The first good news for over three years comes from the shouts of Thais that the prisoners pass on their way to work at the airfields. Charles is accurate with his misgivings about the British public's attitude to the war in the Far East, which became known as the Forgotten War, something that even today continues to rankle with the members of the Burma Star Association.

Letter 164 Ubon May'45
My Darling,

I believe the war in Europe is over. Strong rumours are coming in from the Thais and I am inclined to believe them. If it is, I only pray that Japan packs in because I feel sure the people at home will sit down and treat this war as a side issue. Is it true or not?

Despite the Japanese intention of destroying cohesion amongst the prisoners by separating the officers from the ORs, the Ubon Camp was functioning efficiently under the leadership of RSM MacTavish, Charles Steel and the other NCOs. An unseemly power struggle briefly broke when a group of medical officers attempted to assert their authority.

Letter 165 Ubon May'45

The first real Canteen in the Camp is finished. We have built it as an extension of the Cookhouse to my own design.

There is ample counter space, an office, store and sleeping quarters, besides a neat cookhouse. The Canteen embodies all the best points of previous canteens. We are quite comfortable, but I am worried about the fruit situation.

There is a serious difference between ourselves and the MOs, the only commissioned officers in Camp.

It started off on the move up here, when the MOs behaved in anything but an officer-like manner. The next clash came when I refused to serve an officer in front of a long queue of work-weary men. The Hut WOs have also had differences over the lateness of MOs on sick parades. The upshot of it all is that the SAO – a major – has threatened us all with Court Martial etc. We are carrying on as usual. This is an ORs Camp run by the WOs and there is going to be no 'I'm an officer' business.

We are recognised by the Nips – not the MOs. The trouble is that they have one thought only – themselves. A more selfish lot of upstarts I've never seen. Fortunately, Col.Toosey had a talk with me before he left. His last words were, 'Beware of the Medics – they have no idea of administration'. So we know where we stand.

There will be no Court Martial today, tomorrow or any day . . .

Charles describes the trials of running the canteen, cheating the Japanese and keeping a cool head.

Letter 166 Ubon June'45
My Darling,

A first class 'do' with the Nips today . . .

Since being here I have had to make 100 dollars a period profit for the Nips POW Sports Fund. This is meant for us but the Nips buy their own things out of it. At the same time I have to give information regarding the amount spent per man per month. The total spent by the men in April and May was no less than 20,000 dollars more than they were paid by the Nips.

And so, this afternoon I was called upon to explain where the money came from. Of course I know. Men go out on work parties, steal anything that comes to hand and sell to the Thais. A stick of solder will fetch 20 dollars in this impoverished land, a pair of shorts about 50 dollars. The Nips can't put anything down and be sure of finding it again. At Hashinokos at Nong Pladuk, someone sold the air raid siren during an air raid!! Nails bring about 20c each! And all this in spite of a threat of shooting if caught talking to the Thais.

Many of the men have a great deal of money, although the official IJA orders say that if a WO or NCO is found with more than 20 dollars or a Pte with 10, there will be trouble. They make hundreds and spend it. The Japs then pick up the Canteen receipts and compare it to their payments in wages. The result: trouble!!

At Nong Pladuk, the Officers used to rely on the argument that parties coming through the Camp on their way to Nakompaton Hospital Camp used to spend their money. There, too, the officers were allowed 50 dollars and one could always say that a lot of them had spent it all at once.

Here I took the line that men had saved money at Nong Pladuk for the journey up here (the total surplus spent was less than that which the men could have legitimately brought here) and owing to the Canteen being very small in March, they were unable to spend it, with the result that the surplus appeared in April and May.

Lt. Oda knows where the money comes from. He also knows I know he knows. But one cannot come out into the open and admit anything or otherwise there would be a witch hunt and the men would suffer. And, after all, although the men mainly think about their own stomachs and pockets this stealing is really a mild form of sabotage.

It was a case of Greek meeting Greek this afternoon and honours were divided. I find that in a stand-up of this kind, it is essential to keep still – say, with one's hands behind one's back and not to move backwards. Most important of all is to *keep calm. The Jap method of bullying by shouting is inclined to upset people if they do not preserve a calm attitude and be prepared for it.*

It is useful to stare them out, too, but this sometimes infuriates the little men to the extent when describing one Jap to another, never to question them – which one finds oneself doing automatically – or the fact that he wears glasses. Needless to say, one doesn't mention protruding teeth or slit eyes . . .

One Nip came up to me once, rolled up his trousers and showed me his thighs, saying 'I'm not yellow as you are told, am I?'

Charles had to endure more annoying Japanese antics regarding the canteen.

A typical Nip trick yesterday.

At about 6pm, the 'A side' Gunza sent for me – told me that the Canteen had to clear out of its building by the next morning, because he wanted our building for a new Nip cookhouse. I was furious. The grand little stoves made of home-made bricks, which we have in the canteen have attracted them, I think.

We had to move to the other end of the camp – into one end of a normal sleeping hut. This morning I got hold of a small working party to get the hut or, at least, the end four bays of it – turned into a makeshift canteen.

At about 4pm, Lt. Oda came up in a terrific rage. He, apparently, knew absolutely nothing of the orders given me by the 'A side' Gunza, since the Canteen is his 'pigeon'. Unfortunately, he exploded at the wrong person and I had to get an interpreter before he would cool down. He afterwards admitted to me that, if a Nippon WO ordered me to do a thing, even shifting the Canteen, then I had to do it.

This is typical of the Jap Army. One department does a thing, which is completely opposite to the other. A private soldier in one department will override the ruling of an officer from a rival department. It is no use being told to build a hut by the officer commanding the camp unless one gets on the right side of the

Korean in charge of bamboo. Again, when a Nip is on guard,
he is a direct representative of the Emperor and can do almost
what he wants. I saw a Nippon Sodjo (WOII) slapped by a
Korean private at Nong Pladuk, because the former didn't bow
properly . . .
We are now busily organising this new canteen.

Charles had even become involved 'minting' the prisoner's
currency.

When I get back to England – and things seem brighter now –
I shall be one of the few people who have issued their own
currency system.
I took over the Camp Mint at the same time as the Canteen
and spend a certain time each day in signing fresh cardboard
tokens, as old ones wear out.
At the moment, there is about 1,000 dollars in 20's and 10's
and 5 cents in circulation. These are necessary, because of the
paucity of metal Thai currency.

With defeat after defeat, the Japanese were becoming increasingly nervous that their thousands of prisoners might be
organized by the Thai underground or act on their own to try
and overthrow their captors. Security became tighter and the
guards more vigilant.

Letter 169 Ubon July'45
My Own Wife,
Restrictions are getting tight every day. I am afraid I cannot
write letters so regularly as usual, as they are now have to be
done at night and then re-buried. The Japanese civilian
interpreter now searches one hut at the slightest provocation
and prowls round the camp at all times, appearing here, there
and everywhere.
I have established cordial relations with him, but wouldn't
like to test them. He loves bullshit and we bow and salute each
other half a dozen times when he comes in. He loves to be

thought important and it doesn't hurt to play up to him, if the camp benefits by it.

Almost as if he knows that he is within sight of being freed, Charles reflects on how he has survived. Without doubt, Charles made a conscious decision to adopt a goal that would not only be a record of his imprisonment but, more importantly, keep him in contact, if only within himself, with his young wife. It is a fact that survival, under long-term stressful conditions, is related to adopting a moral initiative, setting a target to aim for, keeping the mind stimulated, adapting to the reality of camp life and keeping a sense of self-pride. Charles chose to follow all these criteria, even to the point of daily shaving and grooming himself.

Letter 170 Ubon July'45
My Dearest Girl,

Nearly 3½ years of captivity!! We cannot understand how we have survived it. I think the only explanation is that those of us who still survive, and I believe 20,000 Europeans as well as countless Tamils, have died on the Thai-Burma railway alone, have to thank the possession of some motive positive, some reason to exist, some power to carry on, that others haven't got.

I am exceptionally fortunate. My body has stood up to the ill winds of the last three years with great success. I have had dengue once, malaria three times, three months of acute diarrhoea and that awful deficiency disease which caused all those sores and affected my legs and eyes. These illnesses are nothing compared to what many have had. Nothing at all. Absolutely nothing. You would realise that if you could see the sights I have seen. For my bodily strength, I can only thank my parents.

But besides physical fitness, there must be a will to carry on. Thousands of officers, in excellent health, have spent their time on their backs. The evergreen joke is to refer to operations taking place in hospital. Upon enquiry, one hears that the oper-

ations are to remove bamboo from officer's backs where they have become embedded.

You know what I am going to say now. I am going to tell you that you are the reason I am still alive, still taking part in administration, still shaving, still cleaning my nails, still folding my much-patched clothes. I am coming back to you not much the worse for wear. I'd even brush my hair, if I had any to brush.

Books have played a great part in my life as a POW. Not Red Cross books, of course – we didn't get those – but books, which were in the possession of men when they became prisoners. I didn't have one until Bukit Timah. This meant that one did not read, because all changes were swops.

I then saw a WO, with whom I was living, tearing up a book for lavatory purposes. I got him to let me have it and changed the remains for a dilapidated 'Reader's Digest'. By the time I moved to Thailand, I had a full size volume called 'B.U.N.C'. At Changkai, I got an omnibus volume of the Rodney Stone stories (Conan Doyle). This I then split into Two volumes. At Nong Pladuk, at one time, I had 'My Mystery Ships' and 'The Big Blockade'. One of these I changed for a volume of six Reader's Digests. Again, this I split into three volumes of two books each and had them bound. So for nearly a year, I have never been without reading matter for any lengthy period.

This has made a great deal of difference to me.

I wish the Red Cross could send books to us. I should welcome books on specific subjects. We simply cannot study anything.

Letter 172 Ubon July'45
My Dear,

For the first three years of captivity, the only clothing I have had from either the IJA or the Red Cross has been a ballbag from the Japs. Excuse the bluntness, but if I called it a 'Jap-happy', you wouldn't understand. . . . it's merely a plain piece of black cloth with tying strings at one end; one places it between the legs and threads the longer tape through the end in front, then tie both tapes.

The Japs wear these as pants – hence 'Jap-happy'. Our people are now forced to wear them without shorts – they haven't any.

Hardly a pleasant sight for a modest, young Thai maiden as the working parties go out!! I'D LOVE TO SEE YOU IN ONE . . .

My Darling,

This is about pets The first pet which appeared in my POW life was a bull terrier bitch, named Peggy. I first saw her on Singapore Island and later met her at Tamarkan, where she was looked after by the Gordons and had two puppies – Speedo and Resto. She accompanied the troops right up country, came down and was bayoneted by a Nip at Nong Pladuk. She was saved and nursed back to health by a POW, came east with us to Ubon and, some weeks ago, delighted everyone one by having sexual intercourse with a boyfriend in the middle of the parade ground during Roll Call. The result is eight delightful puppies, who are now toddling round. She really is a grand dog who has stuck with the troops right through and hates the Nips.

At the Canteen at Nong Pladuk, we had Nigger – an all black female cat. She had the broken stump tail, like all cats in this part of the world. She was a wonderful mother and seemed to enjoy producing family after family. When we last saw her, we had got her as far as Bangkok en route to Ubon. She was again in an interesting condition and went off to look for a quiet corner to drop 'em. We couldn't follow – she went her own way. She had some fine kittens – especially Itchi – who helped us pass the time away.

Shortly before we left Nong Pladuk, a Nip came across with a large male, uncastrated monkey. It had been made savage by the teasing of the Nips (they are as bad with animals as they are with POWs), and male monkeys are notoriously bad if not 'doctored'. He wanted to leave it with us as he was going away. The monkey was a swine. We have to feed it, but it preferred small lumps of human flesh. It got me alright – in the wrist. I soon got rid of that fellow.

At Ubon, there were two monkeys at large, both tame and

castrated. They were merely a nuisance, but hardly deserved the death one of them got at the hands of the Koreans. The other was smuggled out of the camp to safety.

The mynah bird is like a starling. It can learn to talk better than a parrot and there were two tame ones at Nong Pladuk. Here, there is one of a different variety, with a bright yellow hood round its neck. A Nip killed one at Nong Pladuk.

Chicks seem to be the most popular pets here. We have one named Nelson – he had only one eye. His special like is dust-baths. He will lay down and thoroughly enjoy dust being thrown over him.

One of the Nip Sgt. Majors has a pet squirrel – or rather a tree rat. I should like one myself. One or two people had parakeets at Tamarkan.

The tensions of a long confinement with men with whom Charles had nothing in common were released in verse form, which combined to be both outspoken and funny. There was a coolness between the Territorials and the old sweats of the Regular army and Charles made little secret of his contempt for a certain type of soldier.

Letter 173 Ubon July'45
My Darling,
The part played by the regular soldier during our period inside the wire has not been a very glorious one. Querulous, critical, undisciplined and a fear of the Nip has marked him out as a person whom one can't rely on.

This poem – based on Kipling's 'If' – rather hits the mark.
   If you're tattooed on breast and back
   With serpents or the Union Jack,
   If your whole world lies in the brick
   Of Aldershot or Catterick,
   If you have not guts to live
   Your own life – are content to give
   Years of grumbling service to
   A vast machine that thinks for you.

If you can hold to what you've got
And let the other fellow rot.
If you can double in the queue
When other folk are hungry, too.
If you have learned the way to shirk
And swing on mates the dirty work
If you're loud mouthed and love to boast
While others stand but at their post.
If every second word you say
Begins with F and ends with K.
If you can say the obvious things
As though you had the wit of Kings.
If you only care for things you know,
And keep the conversation low,
And brag of brothels and whores
On drunken brawls on foreign shores
If every woman that you spy
You measure with a lustful eye
And only shy at raddled legs
 Toothless and scratching through their negs
If everything that wears a skirt
Is fitting subject for your dirt
If you would up and short your wife,
Because she led your kind of life
If your feelings quickly fray
When discomfort comes your way.
If you know best and won't be told
Just because your number's old.
If your only repartee
Is 'Get some service in, like me'
If you despise civilians who
Have learned your job as well as you
And do it in about as long
As you would take to learn this song
Then there's no doubt that what you are
YOU'RE JUST ANOTHER REGULAR.

The pressing subject of correspondence was once again aired.

My Darling,

How unsatisfactory these 25 word post cards are! It is just like a starving man having a lump of bread put in his mouth and just as rapidly withdrawn.

I have had several from you and sent you back one – at the beginning of this year. My chief trouble is to know where to send it. We hear alarming reports about V1 & V2 from the Japs. If things are so bad, does it mean that Greenway Gardens and Parsonage Lane are no more? Are you still in Liverpool? The safest address, I suppose, is York, but the Windbys may have moved and the present occupants not know you.

Meanwhile, let me thank you for your letters – and especially the full length ones you were able to send before the 25 word limit was imposed. They are glorious in their sincerity, their feelings and their thoughts; they have reached my heart – the destination that you intended. Lift up your eyes and you will quite clearly see that through the mists of the present, the sun of the future must surely shine!

I shall always remember these letters: I shall always save them. I shall always love you.

Chapter 12

Liberation

Letter 176 Ubon, Thailand July'45
My Dearest,

The working parties are bringing in very insistent rumours that the war is over. The Thais, however, who shout messages from behind bushes etc., speak very bad English and have no idea of tenses. 'War finish', may easily mean that the 'war will finish shortly'. The IJA, however, have been saying, 'War finish squashi', too.

There was something funny going on. At the aerodromes, men were now digging holes and trenches across the new runways they had just made. There was now a sense of anticipation in the air. Rumours were rife about the war being over, but camp life still went on the same, with the Japanese showing no signs of relaxing their attitude towards the prisoners. By August, however, it had become obvious that something was about to happen. Even with the real prospect of being freed, Charles recorded his misgivings about what sudden freedom could bring to the camp.

Letter 180 Ubon August'45

My Beloved, we have often talked about what would happen at the end of the war. At one time our few pessimists wondered what would happen if the Nips won. I know . . . we should never have gone home, but should have lived out our days as a slave gang.

It was what would happen after the only possible result that really entertained our minds then – and now. I say then, because it was at Changi that we last talked about it. I say now, because all these rumours point to one thing – the approaching end of the war. Even the Nip MO – a socialist – is reported to have said that it will be only a little while longer.

Shall we be told by the Nips? Will the Japanese behave properly or, in a fit of spite, attack us? How will our people find us? If the Nips cease to feed us, will the Thais (also technically at war with us) feed us or give us credit to buy food?

If they throw open the gates, a majority of men will be both drunk and have VD by the time our people find us. They have been held in too long to listen to reason and are too near the whores and sake shops of Ubon. Very worrying, you must admit.

The issue of clothing also gave a hint that something was about to happen. I have received a pair of Thai-made shorts from the Nips. This now makes two articles in 3½ years, and none from the Red Cross. I was extraordinarily fortunate in buying a towel t'other day. A towel is a very great luxury, you know. For handkerchiefs, I have found the bottom of a mosquito net very satisfactory. I still have a pair of socks, although I don't use them. It would be nice to get some proper clothing again. I still have the little leather stamp wallet which you sent me from Brighton and – even more valuable – the white 'size ring' which you sent me when I was buying your wedding ring. Don't laugh, I am incurably sentimental where you are concerned.

The fever of anticipation finally broke on 15 August, but not before the captors made plans to celebrate the anniversary of the Fall of Singapore at the expense of the prisoners.

Letter 181 Ubon August 1945
My Dearest,

The Japanese are holding a big celebration on the 15th – the 3½ year anniversary of the Fall of Singapore and the 3rd anniversary of the beginning of POW administration <u>We</u> are to 'celebrate' with a Sports Day. I know these Sports Days. Everything is arranged beforehand, but on the actual field itself, the Nips suddenly take charge, cancel half the events, use the equipment themselves and finish by getting drunk.

The Nips are also putting on a Concert in their own quarters, For this purpose, they are using a lot of the large quantity of Red Cross clothing they keep for themselves. I know one Sodjo is having a robe made from Red Cross towels, while dozens of blankets have been sewn together for backcloths. Both these articles are badly needed in the Camp. All Nips on the POW staff are now wearing shorts – plainly marked "Made in South Africa"!

Incidentally, I hear that at the Nip Air Force workshops yesterday, the Nips were busily destroying Red Cross clothing and boots, which they got from this camp. The Nip Navy, who were on Setutai aerodrome, have gone off in a hurry.

Letter 183 Night of Aug 15 1945

I have every reason to believe that the war is over!

I saw the Nips on parade this evening and later saw a friendly Korean come into Camp under cover of the Cookhouse. He said the war was over and kept on talking about some bomb, which we are using on Japan. I <u>do</u> know that the Nips cancelled the Sports Day today and would give no reason, except that they were in mourning.

I cannot sleep tonight. Incidentally, there are no guards coming round. There are normal working parties tomorrow. The men do not, of course, even consider the war over – they have heard this many times before. Some outside parties are coming back.

Putting all these things together, and having seen the Korean *informer myself, I really think that it is time this time. Incidentally, as I write this, I can hear the Nips driving lorries out of the Camp. There is much movement of transport on the road, too.*

Oh God – I hope it's true!!

The following day was momentous for Charles and his long-suffering comrades.

Letter 184 Saturday 18 August 1945
My Darling,

It is true! Oh God be praised, this time it is true!

Major Chida announced the end of the Greater East Asia War on Roll Call tonight. He didn't say who had won, but we know, we know. He was very dignified and pathetic. At the concert, which was due to take place afterwards, everyone was terribly excited. Then at the end – the inevitable happened. We stood and sang 'God Save the King'. You can have no idea how it felt to sing the familiar words, which have been forbidden with the threat of death for over three years. Then came the Dutch National Anthem. People were moved to tears. The singing sounded more like a fervent hymn than anything else.

So, my dear, at last it is over. There is every possibility now of you reading these letter very soon. I see that I managed my object of one per week – 3½ years, that is 182 – and you have two over. At times, I was behind my average, at times in front . . .

Our link with each other has not been broken. Tomorrow, I shall write you my first letter as a free man. Soon I shall be writing you daily letters again . . . Soon our letters won't be necessary. Soon we shall be together again . . . Soon we shall be laying in the darkness once again, my arm around you, your shoulder tucked under my arm . . . Soon we shall be happy beyond all measure.

For Colonel Toosey and the other officers at Nakhon Nayok, the news of the war's end was broken on the 17th. Peter Fane was present when Toosey was told and recalled the exchange between Toosey and Captain Suzuki.

> *'Do I understand that the war has ended?'*
> *'Yes, that's right.'*
> *'That's excellent. Who won?'*
> *'Nobody, it was a draw.'*
> *'Fine, draw or not, we shall do no more work and we demand treble rations as from tomorrow. Tell your guards to keep away and clear out of the camp.'*
>   (Peter Fane IWM 99/43/1)

After the parade that Toosey called to announce the news, the officers also spontaneously sang the National Anthem, 'Land of Hope and Glory' and 'Jerusalem'. The confusion and chaos caused by the surrender meant that there was a lengthy delay before the officers were able to reach the camps housing their men. Toosey journeyed to Bangkok and met up with Boon Pong and Peter Heath, who had been running the clandestine organisation that had been supplying drugs to the prisoners.

After an understandably emotional celebration, Heath was able to organise a one carriage train to take Toosey the 300 miles to Ubon to be reunited with his command. Charles began to write what he called 'Weekly Dailies' to Louise.

> *No.1 Ubon 19 Aug. '45*
> *My Darling,*
>   *An aeroplane passed over the Camp today and dropped some leaflets at Ubon. Last night, after the concert, I was called to the Nip office and was there until about 2am setting up the Canteen arrangements. I asked for the profits paid to the IJA to be returned. As we owe the IJA more for purchases made than they hold in profits, there is no doubt that we shall not be the losers. I also asked that I should be allowed to go to Ubon myself in future for purchasing.*
>   *This morning I went down to the Nip lorries to find Lt. Oda to get permission to go out. After a while, all the Nip officers*

arrived back from the brothel, where they had spent the night. They were in foul tempers and – to put it mildly – I was not successful in getting to Ubon!!. Nor were the MOs, who have now come out of hiding.

The senior MO has now claimed to be Camp Commander instead of RSM MacTavish. A Dutch Lt. has replaced Udg. Scoptabaum (sic. S.J. Slotboom), who has done good service. The people, who were scared to put their fingers in the pie, when it was hot, are now attempting to wade in up to their knees.

Although the war was ended, the Japanese were still present and Charles could not shake off the suspicion that things could still go wrong. Typically, he still kept his own counsel.

Weekly No.2 21st Aug.

Two men were allowed to go to Ubon today – the Cookhouse WO and a Dutchman. While they were there negotiating for credit in order to get increased food for the cookhouse, a Thai officer came up to them with a note, which said that two British officers were nearby. We are not passing this on to the Troops, because it is our experience that, sooner or later, some benighted private tells the Nips.

Cryptically, he added;

There are going to be some interesting revelations very shortly.

Unbeknown to the prisoners, the Allies had parachuted a group of secret agents into the area six months previously. They were part of a SOE Special Unit called Force 136 (Siam Country Section) and their mission was to contact the local units of the Thai Army. Between them, they had trained a guerrilla unit, as well as providing intelligence and pinpointing targets for the RAF. There were a total of seventeen SOE agents in Thailand, as well as units of the American OSS, who trained an underground army of 10,000 Thais. In the event it was just as well that this force was not used, as the British could not have backed them up with their own stretched forces and the Japanese would have crushed them.

With no Allied forces in the country, these secret agents proved invaluable in getting food, drugs and supplies quickly into the camps. Initially, they were the only authority who could negotiate with the Japanese and persuade them to keep clear of the prisoners.

> *Weekly No.3 23 Aug.*
> *My Darling,*
> *I have the whole story, but am sworn to secrecy until the Nips clear off. It is almost impossible to believe, but nevertheless true.*
> *Listen:-*
> *Down at Ubon – 9 kilos from here – are – and have been two British Officers and two British Sjts for the last six months! They parachuted into Thailand six months ago and have been living, unknown to the Japs, in the Thai Military HQ, with a radio in direct contact with Calcutta and Ceylon! This is breathtaking. One is a Major of the Royal Horse Guards (Lt.Col.David Smiley MC) and the other a Parachute Major (actually Major Griswold of the OSS/USAF). Their mission was to train Thai guerrillas for a revolt, which was to coincide with the invasion of Thailand, Malaya and the Netherlands East Indies on 9 September. We were to be armed . . . They actually operated landing strips in the jungle in the north of Thailand, where Dakotas landed and took Thai troops to India for training!*

Charles rather wistfully adds;

> *I wonder what a Dakota looks like?*

Charles and his fellow prisoners were going to have to get to know about many changes that had taken place during the past three and a half years, including new equipment used by the

Allies. Amongst these were the three standard workhorses, the Douglas DC-3 Dakota and the Willys Knight Jeep and the Sten gun.

> *To look back over the last six months in camp and to mention things, which I could not, while we were prisoners.*
>
> *We were aware of a local organisation that intended to revolt against the Nips. Several times we received notes from nondescript Thais, which said, 'Do not act now – wait', and others, which could hardly be read. Once we had a request for the numbers in the Camp. On another occasion, we were asked for conditions in the Camp. This note the RSM answered in the Canteen, while I stood guard outside the door. We now hear that this note got to Lord Louis Mountbatten's HQ in Ceylon, where it was said to be an attempt on the part of the Japanese Secret Service to spread false information about conditions on POW Camps . . . !*
>
> *We did not realise, however, that the revolt was going to be nationwide and led by British Officers. We knew it would be dangerous for us – especially if the Nips got wind of it and attempted to kill us off, before we got arms from the Thais or RAF.*
>
> *For this reason, everyone was ordered to dig shallow pits under their bamboo platforms, so that the Nips couldn't sweep the huts with machine gun fire. We told the Nips it was in case of air raids.*
>
> *We have been very lucky in missing this spot of trouble.*

Weekly No.4 25 Aug
My Dear,

> *Several things have happened in the last few days. There has, of course, been no work. A small party is allowed by the Nips to go to Ubon to collect rations, which the Thais have allowed us to have on the credit of the British Govt.*
>
> *I have issued a statement with reference to the winding up of the Canteen. A news service has been started with news from a radio set in Ubon. We can't understand half the abbreviations*

*– SEAC, Pluto Pipeline etc. The RAF have dropped some fairly
recent newspapers and a summary of the six years of war. I am
very worried over the possible damage done by the V1 & V2.
Food is now much better.*

*I shall never feel free until I am out of Thailand: but best of
all:-the parachutists in Ubon broadcast my name to Calcutta
with the RSM's and others on the Camp staff. I do hope you
hear about it.*

Nearly a week after hearing of the surrender, Charles was over-
joyed to receive his Commanding Officer back.

Weekly No.5 Sunday 26 Aug
My Dear,

*We are overwhelmed today, when Lt.Col.Toosey – who has
done more for POWs than any other officer, came into Camp.
He had commandeered a special train in Bangkok to get to
us. He had with him several officers. We, who have been
running the Camp for the last seven months, feel a great load
of responsibility lifted from our shoulders. It is good to have
real officers, at last.*

*He is in grand form and gave us much heartening news. I
think we shall all be away in 14 days. I believe the Red Cross
boasted that all the POWs in Italy were home in three weeks.
We'll judge them on their form out here, having seen nothing
of them for 3½ years.*

*The Nips here have given us the Red Cross goods, which they
have left. We see little of them (the Japanese) now. The four
Americans in the Camp leave for Bangkok on Tuesday. The
Nips say that they expect we shall be flown out of here. I hope
so – the quicker the better.*

*One fly in the ointment. A large party of men with one MO
left Nong Pladuk shortly before we did. They went to Nakom
Paton to dig ditches. We now hear that they were sent down to
Mengui. At the finish, of the whole 1,000, 250 were dead and
250 seriously ill. We had a number in that party and I should*

have gone myself, if I had not been earmarked to take over the PRI. A narrow escape at the end!

Toosey's arrival was marked by a parade organized by RSM MacTavish. The Special Service men were guests of honour and Colonel Smiley was invited to inspect the assembled ranks of ragged and emaciated men.

Weekly No.6 27 Aug

A great day! This morning the Secret Service people, both Thais and British and Americans came out of hiding. They rode up to the Camp (armed with the new Sten guns!!) and came on parade, where we were all assembled. The Union Jack, the Australian flag and the Dutch Tri-colour were run up. These brave men were introduced to the POWs, who promptly broke ranks and mobbed them! They could not be rescued for hours.

At lunchtime, I fitted up a table and boxes in the Canteen and the RSM, Cookhouse S/Sjt, the WO acting as Adjutant and myself entertained the two Sjts to the best dinner ever seen at Ubon POW Camp! They must have thought we were completely mad by the questions we asked.

For instance, we had been told that Queen Mary had met with an accident and had died. This apparently is not true. Checking up the dates, we learnt that the liner 'Queen Mary' had had a collision off South America about then. And so on.

England sounds a very hungry place, peopled by poorly dressed civilians and much be-medalled servicemen. The girls seem to have made themselves cheap by throwing themselves at the Americans. One Sjt said that there is more VD in England now, than in any other country. Also, that illegitimate children are soaring in numbers. He said that 24% of the unmarried women are pregnant or have had offspring. This is rather unpleasant, if his figures are true.

The RAF have promised to drop papers and a food supply, but we haven't seen anything of them yet. A number of men have broken out of camp and got drunk in Ubon.

Weekly No.7 29 Aug

One of the parachutists yesterday told us that we must lose that 'glassy stare', which he says we all have.

We have got a radio from Ubon and it is operated at the Canteen every evening. This is the first radio I have heard for 4 years. The girls' voices, I'm afraid, give one naughty thoughts. There is a special every evening for released POWs from Delhi.

At last, Charles felt it was completely safe to reveal the true nature of his activities.

Weekly No.8
My Dearest,

Louise I intend to tell you in this letter what I have not dared tell you in the ones I wrote in captivity.

During the last seven months I have been doing a double job. Officially – from the IJA point of view, I was running the Canteen. Unofficially, and in disobedience of IJA orders, I was making money for the Camp.

The Japanese viewpoint toward the sick is different to ours. The Japs say that a sick man is non-effective. Whether in their army or to us POWs they do not pay him and give him a lower ration scale. He doesn't work, so he doesn't need feeding so much. Now the British view is different. We aim at getting the man better, even at the expense of the community.

Up till the IJA took over the Canteens in Sept'43, the profits were devoted to the Hospital in almost all Camps. When the IJA took over the Canteens, they said that no profits must be made. Then the fun started.

While the officers were at Nong Pladuk, Mr.Fullerton 'cooked' the accounts and he and I looked after the Camp Funds, which were buried in a tin can about 18 inches below the surface. We used to 'operate' after dark with the Canteen staff round the Canteen at strategic points. We also had 200,000 dollars worth of illegal drugs and medicines hidden. These were invaluable during the air raids, when morphia smuggled in from the Chinese helped many a poor fellow out. The Nips never found us out.

When the officers left, this underground organisation for welfare was handed over to me. I continued the same system, helped by two trusted Bombardiers, until we moved. I then distributed the many thousands of dollars to the men and told them I would collect it back at the other end. I got nearly all of it back. Here, determined not to get caught (as I heard the fellow at Tamwa had), I prepared a super 'hidey-hole', which would not be disclosed, even if the Canteen was dug up in a search.

This was very satisfactory, until the rains came. The water level rose very rapidly and one night, I was horrified to find the bundles of notes saturated in water! I spent the whole of the next day 'frying' notes on a hotplate over a fire, while a guard kept watch around the Canteen. I then had a waterproof tin made at the tinsmiths and sunk this in water in a different place. That tin, now empty, is still dry.

All accounts had to be kept in duplicate. The true account for ourselves, the 'cooked' ones for the Nips. At Nong Pladuk, we made roughly 60 dollars a day for the Hospital; here, about 50 dollars. Those clever little men didn't find us out.

We had a narrow escape once, though. The RCMS (Worth) came up one afternoon to check the cash. Unfortunately, the day's profit had not been removed. I honestly thought it was CWS for Bangkok Jail, toute suite. By a lucky chance, I remembered he had a sweet tooth and turned him away from the office for some new toffees. By the time I got back, the money was dead correct.

Thank goodness all that is over. It is apt to be rather wearing at times.

Now he was free to reveal his secret hiding places, Charles described the ingenious methods he used to hide his considerable correspondence to Louise and other forbidden materials.

While I am on the subject of deceit, I may as well mention some of the 'hidey-holes' I found invaluable.

I bought a broken gold Waltham watch some months ago from a hard up officer. This I kept underground, but carried it in a false-bottomed sugar tin during moves. My pen, I carried in a rubber pillow, which I slit and scooped out, sticking the hole up again. My pencil, I carried in a secret pocket in the back of a jacket.

Money was carried in a variety of places. The Nips never found out the following places:-The shoulder straps (of a shirt, split open and sewn up again.

The bottom of a haversack, split and sewn up again.

Notes rolled into the centres of home-made cigarettes.

My precious letters to you, my love, came through the move safely with the Japanese accounts! I guess the laugh is on the little yellow boys! Incidentally, I hear that when the officers moved, they packed their highly dangerous wireless set in with a Jap officer's kit and the set was transported by the IJA!!

When the Japs find out about these things, and how the Thai army, officially at war with us, but actually in league with us and was going to revolt, I guess they'll commit hari-kari in mortification.

One of these Special Force sergeants named John Hedley later wrote about his impressions of the British prisoners at Ubon:

There were . . . 1,200 UK, 300 Australian and 1,500 Dutch POWs. Naturally I saw mostly those from the UK, and I have never seen men in finer physical condition. It was a question of the survival of the fittest, and many died. They had a splendid CO in Lt-Col. Toosey DSO, and their discipline, smartness (in spite of the state of their clothes), general bearing and saluting were as good as any I have ever seen. It was obviously his, and his junior officer's leadership and the discipline of the men that had brought them through not only alive but in such superb physical condition . . .

He also made the interesting observation;

. . . that many of them said was that for all the suffering they endured they would not have missed it. I can understand the attitude: to be able to recount experiences few can have gone through, and to have the satisfaction of having overcome such tremendous hardships and difficulties must be a source of pride, and justifiable pride. Another thing which must give a feeling of curious pleasure is to be 'legitimately on the wrong side of the law'.

Charles certainly felt this satisfaction of having 'cooked the books' and got away with cheating the Japanese out of a small fortune. Most prisoners had become skilful thieves and devised ingenious methods of hiding their booty. Forbidden articles like radios, for which men risked beatings and sometimes death, were kept in specially modified objects like water bottles and broom-heads. With liberation came a sense of pride.

Colonel Toosey and Colonel Smiley were concerned that the large numbers of Japanese in the area were still fully armed. After a visit to the Japanese HQ, it was agreed that the soldiers should hand in their weapons and remain in their barracks. Through Smiley's connection with the Thai administration, a good supply of food and entertainments were laid on for the increasingly restless prisoners.

Weekly 10 Ubon 4 September 1945
My Dearest,

A rather amusing weekend. The Thai Governor sent up, what I presume to be the local Amateur Dramatic Society to enter-tain us with dancing last night.

We expected a troupe of dancers who would be clad in the traditional costumes of old Siam. Instead, the Thais were dressed in spotless white drill suits, while the girls wore frocks and high heeled shoes! On the other hand, they did perform the old dances. There is much slow waving of the arms and hands – snakelike gestures. The man never touches the girl, but pursues her as she slowly makes the round of the stage. Music consists hand claps.

One couldn't help noticing that one girl was very pregnant. She seemed unembarrassed in front of her large audience of sex-starved males.

The other show took place the next night. The local cinema was transported to the Camp. This included an ancient electricity generator, a large white sheet and a big drum. The show started with about half an hour's thunderous banging on the big drum. The films then began, the accompaniment being the drum and a fife. The films were in short reels, dated in the 1920s, and were once in series or order. They were not now in order. They were put on as they came to hand and made a marvelous performance. The hens, seen being devoured by a lion one second is gaily chasing it the next. The heroine dies in one reel, but half an hour later drinks the cup of poison, which lays her low. The lads here gave it the bird properly, but the Thais took it to be applause.

A large number of Thai girls came to the Camp to see the football the other day. Two of them, who are connected with the firm who now supply the Canteen, came to the Canteen and we showed them round. There was also a Eurasian, half Thai, half Dane. These girls are really miniatures. They are rarely more than 4'9", and some are most attractive. The Thai language, dreadful to hear spoken by a man, is very pleasant in the women, as – as you possibly know – there are modulations in scale, unlike European languages. The same word, spoken in three different keys, means three different things. One, therefore, gets a singing effect.

By the way, I hear that the name 'Thailand' is now changed back to 'Siam', so I must use that in future.

The pace of repatriation continued to move too slowly for men who had awaited its arrival for years. The bitterness felt by most Japanese-held prisoners, at what they perceived as official indifference and shame, seems to have its roots in this period when they appeared to have been pushed to the back of the queue. Were these men being blamed for Britain's worst military disaster; the fall of Singapore? Britain was euphoric about the victory against Germany which, because of its direct involvement, had touched the lives of all its citizens. The war in the Far East seemed so remote and interminable that there was a general disinterestedness, particularly after the Americans effectively ended hostilities with the dropping of the atomic bombs. It seemed to the prisoners that they had been forgotten by a nation more concerned with recovering from its struggle against Nazism.

> *Weekly 14. 16 September*
>
> *We have not gone. Men are very fed up, indeed. Over a month now since the end. I am afraid that most of the 'We'll get you out quickly' stuff is merely propaganda for you people at home. I cannot help thinking that the official view is that people here have done nothing for the war effort and the first place for transport home should go to those who have been fighting for the last six years. The Red Cross, of course, can be written off. I wish they wouldn't keep on advertising how many food parcels each man got in German POW Camps. They even put a picture of the contents of the parcels in one book dropped by the RAF. Having done without the Red Cross for the last 3 1/2 years, one can do without them now.*

The remoteness of Ubon Camp meant that it had to be supplied by air, something that added to the prisoner's sense of isolation.

> *Weekly 15. 18 Sept'45*
>
> *A terrific show by the RAF in Consolidated Liberators this morning. They roared low over the parade ground and actually dropped a number of canisters right into the camp. One went through a hut. Another hit a man on the head and chest and put him in hospital as seriously injured case.*
>
> *A number of old newspapers were also thrown out, together with the names of the crew. I always hope to get a note from Ken. These planes are terrific. It must be wonderful to be in action with air support, instead of knowing that everyone of the planes overhead is an enemy machine, as was the case in France*

*and Belgium in 1940 and Malaya in '42. We didn't have one
tank in Malaya, and the RAF embarked as we disembarked on
13 January. Even then, they were in too much of a hurry to
destroy machines, which we found on Sembawang Aerodrome
on the week of the Capitulation.*

*Some of the men from the outside tell us that it is now known
that the campaign in Malaya was intended to be a delaying
action designed to give time to garrison Australia with
American troops. It was always known that it was impossible
to hold Singapore. The reason we – in the 18ᵗʰ Div – were
diverted from our destination in the Middle East, was because
Australia complained that too many Australians and not
enough British were in Malaya; so the 18ᵗʰ Div, trained for the
Middle East and desert warfare, was hurried to Malaya and
thrown into jungle warfare within a month of the end. A
political expedient!! I hope that the 20,000 prisoners who have
died in slavery in Thailand haunt those responsible forever!*

Charles then pays tribute to the man he admires above all others;
Colonel Philip Toosey.

Weekly 16
*I went out for a walk with the Colonel and another officer
yesterday. The Colonel is a great man: he would be a Major-
General at least if he hadn't been behind the wire for 3½ years.*

*His leadership, his optimism, his stubborn defence against
the Japs for 3½ years have helped us tremendously. When the
Japs took him from us for the last seven months, it was his spirit
that kept No.1 Group the best in Thailand. We have had fewer
deaths, less trouble with the Nip, less beatings-up. Even the
Nips admire him.*

*We in the 135 Field Regiment feel that we are lucky in having
a man, who has made such a name for himself throughout the
POW Camps, as our own Colonel. In civilian life he is with
Baring's Bank, Liverpool.*

Weekly 17 19 Sept'45
Look here, Louie, my love,

I wanted to buy you something from Siam, but am pretty well prevented from doing anything spectacular by lack of money. The well known racketeers in Camp – and some who weren't suspected – are now buying local silk at 60.00 ticals per metre. Having run the Canteen for two years, I am believed by the troops to be excessively wealthy, but you know me well enough to know that the only money I have now is what has been saved from my pay. However, the Adjutant of the 135 gave me a nice little present, when he got here from Bangkok and I have managed to scrape together enough to buy you a small present. It was no use buying you one metre or so of silk (even though I should like to see you in undies made from that small amount!!), so I got, what is a very representative product of Siam, a silver belt, which maybe you can find a use for.

Incidentally, I will mention here the normal dress of the Siamese women.

She wears no shoes or stockings, except in town, when she usually uses sandals. The majority of women wear a black, ankle-length sarong; the poorer, cotton ones, the better off, in silk. This is kept up by a metal work belt, again the poorer use wire or steel ones, the better off, silver. Invariably, a white blouse is worn with the sarong. In the case of the better classes, these blouses are European type and caught in or tucked in at the waist. The poorer class do not tuck in at the waist. The very poor and the ancient of most classes in the country, wear no covering on the top part at all. On the head, the poor wear a vast straw structure.

They are very regimented in dress, but in Bangkok, frocks are increasingly worn and, if the normal colour scheme of black and white is adhered to, the sarong usually gives place to a silk skirt – very short.

It is the belt which keeps up the sarong, which I have bought as a keepsake for you. They are priced by weight. This was the best I could afford. I hope you like it.

Since the finish, I have sent several communications to you.

147

I know that an official telegram 'Am safe in British Hands. Hope to be home soon. Waiting', was sent. I have also sent one 10 word cable and one 25 word cable to you, and two letter cards to you and one to Shirley. I now have another letter card given me, which I am going to send to Bow. I know you won't mind.

The long wait caused many prisoners to indulge in the pleasures that had been denied them for three and a half years; drinking and sex. Colonel Toosey was anxious about venereal disease being spread amongst his men by the 'comfort girls' and, through David Smiley's contacts, arranged for 10,000 condoms to be airlifted from Delhi.

Weekly 19 20 Sept.
My Dear Louise,
 We were listening to the radio last night and heard in the news that 32 POWs from Thailand had arrived by flying boat at Poole in Dorset. The announcer then had the audacity to say that, of course, these were the fit ones, the others are not yet fit to travel! Something like a minor riot broke among the troops.
 All are terribly disappointed at being let down by our own Government and about 75% are now drowning their sorrows in 'laus' (very raw spirits) every evening. Of these, I gather about 50% are sleeping with Siamese prostitutes in Ubon, which isn't a very wise thing, seeing that the Japanese Army have been in the same beds for the last 4 years. And 90% of Nips have VD.
 However, the RAF yesterday dropped a whole canister full of french letters and ET sets, so apparently England condones the use of our late enemy's comfort girls in view of her inability to get us back to our wives.
 We are told that the mail from England is at Rangoon. We can hardly read how many of our people have been killed by the V bombings at that distance.
 I'm afraid you are going to find your husband very 'anti' by the time he gets back to England, if we are going to be con-

tinually buoyed up by false propaganda and dropped by realisation and fact. This situation rather reminds me of the last week in the Singapore battle, when we were promised that 'the sky would soon be black with planes'. So it was – 3 ½ years too late.

Weekly 20 21 Sept.
My Dearest,
    A stunning display by the RAF again today.
    A Consolidated Liberator came down low over the Camp, diving down and soaring again, while its crew lined the open doorway and waved. They threw out a roll of newspapers, which crashed through the roof of a hut and some magazines, some of which were unfortunately cut to ribbons by the tail. This is the piece that fluttered to the ground at my feet (a pin-up). Or do you think that one of the crew tore it out of a magazine and dropped it – just to entice us? Darling, am I very wicked if I say that this is one of the nicest pictures I've seen lately?

With discipline beginning to fray at the edges, Colonel Toosey flew to Bangkok to plead his case to allow the Ubon Camp to be evacuated.

The Colonel has gone to Bangkok to see what is happening to the evacuation muddle. Things are getting rather out of hand here. We have no facilities for punishing people and the attraction of women and drink is too much for most men. And once men get sozzled, clashes with the Nips (who are still armed) become likely.
    The Nip discipline is remarkable. I should never have believed it of them. They are actually bringing our drunks into the Camp – and as far as now, their behavior is exemplary.
    I do hope we get news about evacuation soon.

Toosey's visit was successful and plans were made for the Ubon prisoners to be evacuated. Charles's brush with the Australians,

149

who put scorpions in his bed, still rankled and coloured his opinion of the whole country.

Weekly 21 23 Sept.
My Darling,
It looks very much as if we are leaving very soon. Col.Toosey seems to have hurried matters at Bangkok. The Australians have already left – and they're the last lot of Aussies I ever want to see.

The stages of our homeward journey will be by lorry to Ubon, by sampan across the river (now swollen by the monsoon and stretching almost to the station; it took us 10 minutes to cross in February – now it is an hour's anxious voyage!), by train via Koust to Bangkok, by 'Dakota' transport planes over the mountains to Rangoon in Burma, and then by sea to the UK.

Darling, I'd love you to be here and to accompany me on the journey. Nevertheless, I know there will be a letter from you waiting at Rangoon! I'm counting the minutes . . .

With repatriation imminent, Charles now considered the practicalities of meeting up with his wife. The war had caused disruption and families were no longer living at the same addresses as before the soldiers went into captivity. This uncertainty caused much anxiety but the waiting families were kept informed by the authorities and were generally waiting at the dockside for their loved ones.

Weekly 22
I have been thinking a lot about my arrival home. If I do not get communications at Rangoon, I shall be in a quandary.

Say we land at Liverpool or Southampton – the latter more possibly. I shall not know whether Greenway Gardens or Parsonage Lane still exist. I shall not know whether you are still in Liverpool (fairly unlikely, I think). I think the best thing is to go to London and, failing the telephone directory, go a round of the old addresses from somewhere I shall be able to pick up clues and get in touch with you.

We shall receive 8 weeks leave, pending demobilisation plus one day for every month abroad (another 48 days about). How about your demobilisation? If I wasn't a POW, I gather I should be demobilised in Group 25. I should think your number would be fairly low, too.

There seems to be heaps of back pay and gratuity waiting for us, besides several medals. There is only one medal I should like, for which I have qualified and that is the TA Long Service & Efficiency silver medal (12 years or 6 years War Service). Incidentally, you will be one of the very few women in England who is entitled to this medal. I am very proud of you. The other medals they can give to someone who has earned them. We haven't.

If you are still in the ATS, will you be able to get leave, I wonder? I should like you to do so if possible. I want to get back to the City at the very earliest possible moment, the last six years have been wasted; in any case, I cannot countenance having a holiday while my wife is working. We either both have leave or I'm going back straight away. You're the person due for a yasme.

And where shall we meet? Not at Sam Isaacs's corner, I hope. Probably at a railway station? I wonder what rank you have obtained? I do feel terribly miserable at the fact that you have a miserable OR attached to you. I am not going to spoil your success by introducing myself in any way. I am fearfully proud of you, darling! But . . . if you do get a swelled head through reading these remarks, I'll bat it back into place . . . and lay you across my knees as I seem to remember doing once before in play. Dearest Louise, I love you very dearly.

Chapter 13

Home at Last!

Weekly 23 24th September 1945 Ubon Thai Military Barracks
My Darling,

A great day, indeed! Today we rode out of Ubon POW Camp, past a row of Japanese, consisting of Major Chida (CO), his Adjutant, Lt. Oda, the Defence officers – oh, the whole lot of them, plus their WOs & Sjts. As the trucks rolled past, they gravely saluted and held the salute until it was returned by the NCO in charge. This sounds nothing to you, but it was an amazing experience for us, who have had to salute all ranks of Japs and come stiffly to attention and bow to Nip officers for 3 ½ years.

My party consists of 25 men (the complement of a Dakota). The Dutch drove us to Ubon by lorry. We then embarked on the swollen river in the hollowed-out tree trunk sampans of the Thais. About five men to each. These canoes are very fragile. One sits cross-legged and does not dare move, as the freeboard is about 3 inches.

There followed an amazing journey. We crossed the river and then penetrated the flooded country of the other side. We moved along silent waterways and passed through bushes and lanes of trees. It was most eerie. Sometimes the boat had to push its way through the tops of tangled undergrowth. The water was not deep.

We finally arrived at higher ground after 40 minutes of

*fascinating travel. We then marched to the Thai Barracks,
where the Thai guards presented arms as we passed. It is now
raining heavily.*

So began what became a rather leisurely journey back to
England. To their surprise and delight, the POWs were feted by
the Thais as they began their long train journey to Bangkok.

Weekly 24 Korat, Siam 25ᵗʰ September
My Dear,
   *I can only liken today's experiences to the triumphal advance
across France in September 1939 by the I Corps. You remember
my description of that.*

   *We boarded the train – real coaches – at Ubon this morning
and were amazed to find a deputation from Ubon awaiting.
Baskets of flowers, fruit etc !! and pretty Siamese girls to present
them.*

   *We were more than amazed to find that at almost every
station, the same performance was repeated. Generally
speaking, at each end of each platform were Thai police with
British, Thai and US flags. In the centre were massed the
officials of the village, their wives and daughters. On each side
were ranks of school children, all with Union Jacks. And then
the vast population simply teemed wherever it could gain a
vantage point. And the eats!! Masses of coconuts, bananas and
boiled eggs: cakes and coffee: all kinds of things. At some places
we got out, at others the stuff came through the windows. At
one place, I saw the chubbiest Chinese baby I've ever seen. I
took him from his mother into the train – and what a raspberry
I got from the men!! He wasn't more that three months and I
had to be very careful – completely naked, of course. They all
are up to 5 or 6.*

   *Here at Korat, the whole platform is laid out with tables and
chairs. Flags are everywhere. I have just eaten a delicious Thai
meal of curried chicken, plus a kind of spiced mutton and good
coffee and whisky (laus) to finish up with. Some of the banners
are amusing, 'To the victors of our country, welcome',*

'Thai-Chinese welcome you' and one private note of good wishes from, 'The Anti-Japanese Secret Society'! Hosts of individual presents, too: some of the poorest brought rice in banana leaves.

We reach Bangkok tomorrow.

Weekly 25 Bangkok, Siam 26 Sept'45
My Dearest,

I seem to be falling quite naturally into the habit of writing the 'daily' once again. I wonder whether you'll think all these letters worth reading or merely so much nuisance value.

There is a small civil war between the Siamese and Chinese going on here. This is not affecting us in anyway, as we are billeted at the airport under the wing of No.11 Casualty Evacuation Unit of the RAF.

We arrived here this morning and saw our first English girl – a Lt.Col. in the Red Cross, grand daughter of the Duke of Somewhere and ADC to Lady Louie (Mountbatten). She looked as if she was pretty efficient – in bed!

It is great to be in the care of the RAF. No muddle here. Beds are stretchers on frames and there are really white sheets. Food is excellent – to our tastes – although one realises that it is the same old army food out of cans. There is an Indian Bathhouse Unit here, too, but I am rather wary of hot baths at the moment, so went for a magnificent swim in the drain around the paddy field – probably my last swim in the nude.

In the evening, I had the job of issuing free Players and a few odds and ends of Red Cross. We got T$10.00, too, and as this is the last opportunity of spending Thai currency, I went along to an Indian Canteen and blew it on coffee at T$1.00 per glass, a supper costing T$5.00 and the rest on Paradise bananas at 30c each. And a few days ago, one debated whether to spend 20c on an egg for lunch!! Times have changed.

Some Gurkhas near here have killed a couple of Nips on a working party, but an RAF fellow, who hit one, went up on a charge!

The War Criminals Courts have started in Bangkok and yesterday, Lt. Suziki (he was at Nong Pladuk and Kinsaiyok) was shot. Col. Toosey is going to Ubon by plane tomorrow to collect Major Chida and the rest. They are all going to get bullets.

Charles refers to a worrying tendency that affected all released Japanese POWs and that was the uncomfortable gulf that appeared between themselves and non-POWs. It all added to sense of alienation, which took sometime to disappear. For some, it never went away and caused strained relationships and, for some, the breakup of marriages.

Meanwhile, we are awaiting for evacuation by air tomorrow. I am in charge of No.54 plane apparently.

A couple of 'Jeeps' are here. These are most interesting and have apparently been in use some time.

There seems to be an invisible barrier between ourselves and 'free' men. On their part, they are embarrassingly polite and anxious to show unwanted sympathy. On our part, there is a marked inferiority complex and a tendency to shut up like oysters whenever a 'free' man comes along. I hope this wears off.

As each man arrived in Rangoon, he was handed the following printed message.

Welcome to Rangoon !!

At last the day has come. Three years of darkness and agony have passed, and a new dawn is here, bringing with it for all of us deliverance from danger and anxiety, and for you above all freedom after bondage, the joy of reunion after long separation.

Through these long years we have not forgotten you. You have not been at any time far from the thoughts of those even who had no personal friends or relatives among you. We of the Red Cross have tried every way of establishing contact and relieving your hardships. Some provisions have been sent, and many messages despatched; but we do not know how much had reached you, for the callous indifference of the enemy has made this task well nigh impossible.

But now that the enemy is beaten and you are free once more, we are doing all we can to give you the welcome you richly deserve and to make your homeward path a pleasant and a joyful one. If our preparations in Rangoon leave something to be desired, it is only because the end has come sooner than we dared to hope and has found us unprepared. These deficiencies will be more than made up by your welcome in India and your homeland.

On behalf of the Indian Red Cross and St. John War Organization, we welcome you. May God bless you and send you home rejoicing!

Weekly 26 Rangoon, Burma 27 Sept'45
My Dear,

We arrived here this afternoon after an enjoyable 2½ hours flight by Douglas Dakota. The crew were British, the pilots Canadian. The pilots invited me into their cockpit and showed me the workings etc. The navigator also explained the route and maps. We flew over the jungle and, for the most part, above the clouds. We crossed the Bay of Bengal at low altitude and finally made an unfelt landing at Rangoon. Things then happened in double time.

We were whisked away by IASE trucks to a WVS Reception Centre, where peaches and cream, bread and butter were waiting. Great kindness here. From there we moved quickly to the outskirts of Rangoon itself, where we went into No.52 Indian General Hospital. We are now quieter individuals, and not parties of men. I'm afraid units are split up all over the place. I have just been examined and got marked 'Fit for Discharge', but the fool insists on me taking mepachrine and vitamin tablets. These Medical people ought to be suppressed; they have such a good impression of themselves. I saw a talkie tonight and wrote two airmail letters – one to you, one to North Cray folk. Meanwhile, it rains steadily.

Weekly 27 Rangoon 30 Sept'45
My Dear,

I have been able to write airmail letters to you for the last two days, so have omitted these. Yesterday, I got your first letter and answered it straight away. Say, darling, did it give me a kick or didn't it!! I feel like pushing houses over. Being greedy and very much in love with my wife. I wonder if you look differently or whether I do? I am hoping to come home by sea in order to let my hair grow! It looks like a buck navvy at the moment!!

We are getting to know the names of the men who died on the Mengui Road working party (see Weekly No.5). Of the 135th contingent, 17 died of starvation out of 35 and most in the first fortnight of August. After coming through 3½ years of beastliness, it is hard lines for a bloke to die in the last fortnight. I have visited survivors of this party in hospital here (we are now out of the 52 Indian General Hospital and in the No.6 Independent Beach Medical Unit) and find them pretty poorly. However, they have pretty VAD's looking after them, so I expect they'll be alright in time.

I have been into Rangoon twice now. What with Nip bombing, RAF bombing and Nip scorched earth tactics, it is now one vast dung heap as far as I am concerned. I have bought a pair of chaplies. Canteens are poor in the extreme, although in large buildings. Bananas are poor compared to the Siamese passion bananas, but better than the jungle ones.

I have contacted two of the Field Regiments here – the 27th and 139th. The 114, 134, 136, 160 and 304 are also here, I believe. I wonder where the good old 97th is now? The 25 pdr seems to have established itself as the world's finest field gun. Apparently Jeeps are issued instead of motor cycles now. I have seen three films since arriving – all talkies; 'Two Thousand Women', 'Saratoga Trunk' and 'Lady, Lets Dance'. The latter was especially good.

At long last, Charles and his comrades embarked for their journey back to England. Through the insistence of Colonel

Toosey, the 135th returned together as a unit and were not split up as many other units were.

Charles took advantage of sea travel to indulge in a spot of people watching and, as ever, his observations were trenchant. He also felt a fleeting pang of conscience over the huge gulf between the Officers and Warrant Officers and the NCOs and Other Ranks with regards to accommodation and food.

Weekly 28 At Sea, Bay of Bengal 12th Oct'45
My Beloved,

You will notice a break in the continuity of these letters. This due to the fact that on my removal from the Beach Medical Unit to the Transit Camp, I was able to write to you everyday (sometimes more often). Anyhow, I am once more unable to post letters so am continuing my impressions in this form. The further I get nearer home, the less use it will be to post letters.

We embarked yesterday at Rangoon and came down the muddy river in invasion barges. The Orbita *was laying some miles downstream. A brief description of the vessel may interest you. She is about 16,000 tons and belongs to the Pacific Steam Navigation Co. She was built in 1914 and served as an auxiliary cruiser in the last war. In this war, she has been used as a troop ship, but ran aground in the Red Sea a few months ago. This is her first voyage after reconditioning at Belfast. She left Liverpool a month ago and is due back there with us.*

The accommodation for officers and WOs is excellent. We have bunks with mattresses about 9" thick, white sheets, a steward to do the necessary, and wash hand basins etc in the cabins. The mess is grand. The First Class Dining Room (cream paint pillars, concealed lighting, male waiters), is divided in two by a curtain. The officers are on one side, the WOs on the other. The food is absolutely tip top.

The Sergeants are in canvas bunks and feed separately in the Troops' Dining Hall at a special sitting. The men are packed like sardines in the dim depths of the ship, but all appreciate the tiers of bunks instead of hammocks.

This luxury – for that is what it is – has come as rather a shock to us. I wish the difference between the Officers and WOs from the rest was not so great. For breakfast this morning, we had 'Kellogg's' All Bran, a curry, then (we thought we had finished) a great plate of two sausages and four rashers of bacon, bread, butter (help yourself) and marmalade. Fresh milk and sugar ad-lib! Now, the ORs had some unsweetened porridge, one boiled egg, a chunk of bread and butter and 1 pot of tea. Last night, we had apple pie – real apples, mark you!

The WOs and Sjts have a lounge with individual tables and chairs, sofas and – a grand piano! The decks are now marked off and we have the whole of 'A' deck aft, the Officers 'A' deck forward. You have no idea how we feel, darling. This will help us lose our jungly complex in no time. The vessel is not very fast – 14 knots – (the Mount Vernon did 24 knots on her dash to Singapore) and by the time I get home, I promise you I'll be civilised again. Yesterday was a great day. My hair parted for the first time!

There are three classes of people on board who interest us very much. The first is the waiters. These fellows are 17–19. You see, we haven't seen youths of this age for 4 years. Another set who are 'new' to us are the old merchant seamen – grand old fellows, much over the age of the men we have lived with for so long. They are real 'Dads' and terribly father-like to us.

And thirdly, are those little bits of Heaven – the four children on board. These babies of 2–3 were born to civilian internee parents in Bangkok Jail. In spite of this, they look glorious. Their skins are like petals and their hair a mass of winter sunshine. Darling, you cannot imagine what it means to see these tots after the black, naked brats covered with dirt and sores that stumble under one's feet everywhere in the East. They are supreme joy personified.

There are a number of women on board – civilians and IANS sisters. They are pretty miserable specimens and after seeing the superb carriage of the Chinese, Thai and Burmese girls, one can't help feeling ashamed of these fat-bottomed, waddling white women. Thank goodness you know how to walk, darling.

*Thank goodness you have a glorious figure. Thank goodness
you are YOU!*

I will airmail or cable from Colombo, if possible.

The *Orbita* stopped at Colombo for a short stop, during which
Charles and his comrades were served a lunch by WRNS,
watched a film, sent cables home and were kitted out with new
uniforms. The next time Charles put pen to paper was to send
an airmail letter from Egypt.

Airmail 1 SS Orbita *off Alexandria, Egypt 30ᵗʰ Oct'45*
My Dear Girl,

*A most interesting day yesterday, which started at Port Suez
and ended at Port Said. The passage of the Canal took about
13 hours, with a stop in the Bitter Lakes (about half way).*

*The Canal is much as I expected, but the desert on each side
was much more inhabited than I expected. In fact, almost all
along there are military camps and installations by the side of
a railway and a first class road. There is one swing bridge – the
one used, I expect, when the 8ᵗʰ Army came down into Egypt
to check the Germans at El Alamain. The famous 'Desert Rats',
now in Germany, had left a large whitewashed message to
ex-POWs on a wall by the side of the Canal.*

*An interesting sight were two of Italy's largest battleships
moored in the Bitter Lakes and heaps of scrap iron by the side
of the Canal. These were once ships, unfortunately hit by Italian
bombs, while in the Canal and now pulled out of the Canal after
dynamiting. A number of Italian and German prisoners were
also to be seen. These seemed well fed, were clothed completely
and even wore boots.*

*We were at a picture show on 'A' Deck, when a blaze of light
proclaimed our arrival at Port Said. The show was immediately
cancelled and we swarmed to the side. What a sight! Lights
everywhere. A great lean French light cruiser, the British cruiser
HMS London and heaps of destroyers and submarines and
merchant shipping, all blazing with lights. The comments*

exchanged between the sailors on the London and ours were very amusing. One enquiry, which drew a laugh, was when sailor enquired when were we going to hoist our sails – a comment on the Orbita's *staid, old age and respectability. She really does look like an elderly maiden aunt – but, nevertheless, she is getting us to where we want to go.*

A number of officers and ORs of the Women's Mechanical Transport Service are now on board. The ORs, three Sjts and Cpl and L/Cpl are feeding the WOs, but using the Officers' lounge. The Cpls are the biggest girls I've ever seen. I never realised so much girl could be got inside a uniform. By God, they're huge!

Airmail 2 30.X.45
Darling,

This is actually a continuation of my last letter.

We stopped at Port Said for about three hours, but were not, of course, allowed ashore. Troops rarely are, you know, in this sink of iniquity.

As soon as we stopped, dozens of bumboats came out. In each, was an Arab shouting in English, while a native strove desperately to reach the ship. The drill was this. After successfully fighting, ramming and pushing their boat to the steel sides of the liner, the salesman threw up a cord, which he enjoined those on board 'to make fast, MacGregor' (strange, how many natives learn their English from Scotsmen). A basket was attached to the middle of the salesman who held one end and you t'other. The wares were displayed below and conveyance of both money and goods was by this aerial ropeway. At times, it looked as if the Orbita *was anchored by dozens of thin lines. Business was brisk at first, but rapidly tailed off, because people on board with more than 2d are very small in numbers. Prices fell rapidly. The staple industry of all these N.African lands is, as you know, leather goods (camel & kidskins). There are handbags and pouffe covers galore. Fortunately, earlier in the day, I got advance information that we were to receive a further payment (the RAF administration bought a lot of stale beer at Suez and are giving the troops a payment to cash in on it) and I managed to negotiate a temporary loan on the strength of it.*

The handbag I got you is blue and white dyed camel skin – I knew you wouldn't want the natural brown leather. I'm afraid that the inside isn't up to pre-war standards as I remember them, but it doesn't look too bad from the outside and should match the blue and white summer ensemble you told me about. It may see you through until handbags are obtainable in England again.

I was standing by the Squadron Leader, who is doing Paymaster in such a niggardly fashion, when he lost his wallet last night. This poetic justice rather pleased me. He started talking about his hard luck and grew fearfully narked when I reminded him that we should all be poorer together now. The administration (all grounded RAF officers, who don't care a damn) is too appalling for anything – and yet they won't let us take over.

Weekly 29 Off Algiers 3 November 1945
My Dearest,

A lot of water has flowed past the Orbita *since I laid down my pen. The above letter was written when I was 8,000 miles from you – now I am only 1,000 or so. It seems fairly certain that there will be no more opportunities to post mail, so I shall continue my notes in this form.*

The Orbita *is taking a route well clear of the normal trade channels. Between Malta and Gibraltar it is unusual to see land. We have had the coast of North Africa in sight all the way. Over on the port bow, the Atlas Mountains lay, fold upon fold, looking just the same as they did to the ancients who first explored this sea so many thousands of years ago. Bizarta and Algiers showed as clusters of tiny buildings completely dwarfed by the surrounding landscape. I have never seen so calm a sea. The whole area is like a still lake, through which the prow of our vessel cuts – with a swishing sound. Our track can be seen for miles. The water is blue, but not so blue as the Caribbean Sea. Darling, one of my many ambitions is to be able to afford to take you on a cruise or sea journey of some kind. Life on a ship is so utterly divorced from life on land. You would enjoy it tremendously – after the first day or so. It is a fact that the sexes are attracted by each other more while at sea – I think this explains the tangles, which involve the single on voyages. Even under the difficult conditions on this ship, I know that fun and games are going on between the Red Cross 'ladies' and some of the officers. As far as I can see, the Red Cross exists solely to give wartime uniforms to women who haven't the guts to join a useful service and secondly to provide the commissioned ranks with a little feminine company in out-of-the-way places.*

We are now wearing battledress. What with collars and ties for all ranks and black ebonite regimental badges, it is becoming increasingly difficult to tell the 'licentious and drunken soldiery' from the 'officers and gentlemen'. So much so, that some of the girls on board got into conversation with some privates yesterday. It is very difficult for a short woman to inspect a tall man's shoulder insignia. Thank God for the civilian suit, which is gradually drawing closer.

A strange coincidence was revealed when it was discovered that Colonel Toosey had bought his house from the *Orbita*'s captain in 1936. Toosey was also a well-known figure in Liverpool business circles and the directors of the shipping line sent a cable requesting VIP treatment. This led to much socializing during the voyage, which was also extended to the warrant officers. It was during a bout of liquid relaxation that Charles discovered how close he had come to his much sought after commission.

Airmail 3 Off Crete 31.X.45
My Dearest,
Rather a happy morning today. The Col and the Adj sent for BSM Ramsbottom (known as Sheepsarse) and myself, and Lt.Col Knight of the Royal Norfolks sent for his CSM, a very

decent fellow named Peacock (how biological these names!). When we got down to their cabin, we found a passable imitation of an off-licence, with bottles everywhere and a heap of cracked ice in the wash hand basin.

What had happened was this. The Captain of the ship had had a cable from the owners at Liverpool saying that among his passengers was a Lt.Co.Toosey RA, who must be shown every consideration, as he was a personal friend of the directors. The first consideration, which our portly Captain showed was, of course, a plentiful supply of Black and White and every other known liquor, all of which came from the supply allowed the officers of the vessel. Passengers, on the other hand, are only allowed a certain ration of beer. Well, we had a very pleasant morning, although I drank more than I like to, but it is very difficult not to do so when in company like this. I expect you find the same thing. I do hope you haven't developed a craving for alcohol or tobacco, because I have always thought that one of your most charming features was your open-air attitude to life and your power to live your life and enjoy it without the artificial aids which so many have to call in to give them artificial self-confidence and artificial high spirits. And, if one can't assume responsibility without the help of habitual drinking and smoking – well, it is time to drop it.

You must excuse this digression, but I have seen men sink to such low depths when, without a smoke and such terrible results of drunkenness, that I now only drink or smoke when socially necessary. People simply do not realise how great a hold a habit can obtain on them.

Incidentally, during our conversation, the Col apologised for my non-arrival at an OCTU and made the excuse that he had only been in the Regt a month before we sailed and that he was completely overworked during this period. He seemed genuine enough. He is the finest man I have ever met. I have no doubt he would be a Brigadier and probably a Major-General, if he hadn't been thrown away at Singapore.

By the time lunch arrived, the good Orbita, so steady up to now, was behaving like a bucking bronco. However, it calmed

*down after a lazy afternoon in the sunshine on deck and an early
night.*

Airmail 4 Approaching Malta 1.X1.45
Darling Girl,

*The weather is getting colder and the ship is one huge sniff,
cough, cold and sneeze. I found two of my people in their bunks
at inspection time well away with flu, so I bunged them straight
along to hospital. It is dangerous to take risks with malaria
sufferers, in view of the likelihood of Blackwater Fever.*

*Darling, let's clear up a point raised in one of your letters. It
is about the 'altering' business during our separation. I know
at first glance a difference in each other might have taken place
and is likely – after all, for the last four years you have been
mixing with the upper classes and I with the lower – but does
this conclusion bear logical examination?*

*For the first 25 years of our lives we have been living very
much the same lives. We come from similar middle class stock,
we come from middle class families, we were both educated at
secondary schools. We did similar types of work, we enjoyed
similar types of pleasure. Our attitudes towards politics and
religion are similar. Is this quarter of a century of similarity
going to be completely affected by four years of different living?
Of course it isn't.*

*And take another view. One of the most comforting things
which your letters have told me is that you are still in close touch
with our old friends and acquaintances. What is more, you are
hoping to renew those friendships. Would this be the case if you
had altered in any way or if some of your acquaintances, since
you obtained a temporary commission, had blinded you with
the lustre of the upper classes? Of course it wouldn't. To hear
you talking about Iris and Albert, Jack Perkins, George Lane
and the rest, means that you are still the Louie I love and not a
person whose exhilarating experiences of the last four years
have gone to her head. To hear you talk about cooking for the
family is as balm to my soul.*

And, anyway, I have lived, eaten and slept with Officers for the last 3½ years, less 7 months when I did an officer's job.

You see, I am sure that we shall come together quite naturally because I see, quite clearly, a scene in our garden in forty years time. You will be reading these letters and I shall be gardening, and I shall come over to you with the loveliest rose I can find. As I pin it to your shawl, I can see you look up and hear you say, 'Darling, what silly children we were to think that a mere war would alter our love for each other!' And I shall kiss you, because I shall still love you . . . .

This need to reassure each other that everything would be unaltered and that they could pick up the threads of their lives without a problem, hid the worries and doubts that assailed most of the men on the *Orbita*. The long period of separation had put an enormous strain on relationships and many did not survive. Seeking the comfort of fellow victims, 'The Jilted Lovers' Club' sprang up after a batch of recent mail was received.

Airmail 5 In the Gulf of Tunis 2.XI.45
My Dearest One,

I was awakened early this morning to see Pantellaric, the much bombed island, which constituted our first stepping stone across the Med from Tunisia to Italy. I stuck my head out of the porthole and there saw a dark mass of mountains surrounded by a leaden sea. Two lighthouses twinkled. I recovered my head and laid back on the pillow. So that was Pantellaric.

We passed Malta in the darkness and saw only its lighthouse. This morning, after Pantellanic, came Cap Bon, where the Germans staged an unsuccessful 'Dunkirk', while being thrown out of Tunisia. The islands of Zambretta and Zambra were very near. Another fine sight this morning was the P & O Corfu, outward bound with troops. This was the first vessel to arrive in the UK with POWs. Her present passengers are dead quiet and did not answer our shouts and taunts. They did not, apparently, need to be told they were going the 'wrong way'.

Last night THE JILTED LOVERS' CLUB held its first meeting. This organisation came into being after Suez, when it was discovered that about a hundred men had heard that either their wives had been unfaithful or that their girls had married someone else. The Club fortified itself with beers and a pleasant evening was passed singing 'Somebody Stole My Gal', 'Thanks for the Memory', 'Alone' and other applicable tunes. A resolution was passed asking the Captain to turn back to Bali or some other destination where love is cheap, if not free. Everyone seemed in high spirits, and no one could see that tears were not far below the surface.

I hope to post these letters in Gibraltar.

Sweeping Labour gains at the Municipal Elections! Up go the rates. I see that President Truman has made a speech, in which he says that it is essential that American industry is freed from Government control as soon as possible, so that private enter-prise and competition may advance the country's commerce. We in England are doing the opposite thing. Undoubtedly we shall realise our mistake, but how long will that be? And how many markets will America have captured?

I hope the big storm which is raging around the British Isles is clearing up. The Captain said yesterday that the danger of hitting storm-loosened mines is a very real one.

Oo ur . . .

Weekly 30 Off Spain 4.XI.45
My Beloved,

It thrills me to think that at this time next Sunday I shall be with you.

Along our starboard beam is a magnificent sight – the high Sierra Nevadas, with the peaks covered with snow.

The sun catches the white and gives a warning as to what is waiting for us in a European winter. We are well in shore and the fresh wind seems to contain in it the clean nip of the snow.

We reach Gibraltar about 9pm – a great nuisance not getting there in daylight. The difference in the 'growing dark', times seem very strange after our sojourn in areas where darkness falls at the same time all the year round.

The sea is green today and decidedly choppy. The Orbita ploughs through it with scarcely a movement. She is wonderfully steady. Thirty years ago, when she was built, they built deep draughted ships to go _through_ the seas; now they build light shallow vessels to go _over_ the sea in search of speed and yet more speed. The Orbita is as deep draughted as the Queen Mary, although only a 1/5th of her size!

I have got some tins of grapefruit juice for you. This was issued in the Red Sea, where one's blood is liable to get overheated. You must be in need of citrus juices after so long without oranges and lemons etc.

Weekly 31

We pulled into the Bay at Gibraltar, paused long enough for mail to be hoisted on board and went out again straight away. A wonderful sight, Louie, but a nuisance that it wasn't daylight. There was no moon and the dark mass of the Rock could only be seen against the star spangled velvet of the heavens as a black mass, forbidding and grim. Around the base, sending hundreds of gleaming, twinkling fairy lights across the water, was the town itself, glittering lights, which got fewer and fewer as they ascended the hill. Finally, they lost themselves in the blackness, where only one or two lights showed, where gunners kept guard in the passages and tunnels of the Rock itself.

There was not a lot of mail – one for me to be exact and, of course, from your dear self. I had a good laugh at one or two points. Why? I shall tell you.

Do you remember walking through York on our last Sunday? The subject of driving was mentioned and you said you were going to start lessons – that week, I understood. The years pass. On 22 Oct 1945, you blithely inform me that you are about to take your final lesson! I rather saw the funny side of a 4 years driving course. No-it's all right, dear-I'm not puzzled – I realise you must have postponed your course! Now I wonder if it is a civilian or military course? The Nips got my driving licence at Singapore. I wonder whether I shall have to pass one of these tests if I take out another? Anyway, I can't quite see us having a car yet awhile. A house and home comes first on the bill, doesn't it?

The other thing that tickled me was the mention of chocolate. Here am I, studiously saving every issue, buying all I can and generally hoping to give you a sweet surprise and there you are doing exactly the same thing for me. You really are a sweet darling. Louie, don't you think that this little incident is symbolical of all that we intend our married life to be? We both like chocolate. We both know each other likes it, and so we put each other first and, quite in ignorance of each other's actions, do our best to make our partner happy.

I am sorry to hear about Winnie O'Grady, with whom I had a very slight acquaintance. She seemed a decent kid. I note you say '*she* is divorced'. I wonder whether you mean that literally or whether she divorced her husband. I know that there are heaps of matrimonial troubles. Two officers found out that they were girl-less last night. 'The Jilted Lovers Club' had a real session again last night and invited Col. Toosey as honorary member. They successfully drowned their sorrows.

Louie, beloved wife, we've <u>got</u> to make a success of our married life. Failure would be a stigma on each of us, which we should bear for life. There will be difficulties, problems, disappointments for us to face. Let's always pause and look back on the last few years and realise that nothing could be <u>quite</u> so bad or unpleasant or as dangerous as these last few years.

I think our first big problem will be our first home. I think it is essential to get away from the family roof tree as soon as possible. I expect it will be a temporary home, because we are not likely to find the house we want during the great housing shortage. What do you think? Have Iris and Albert their own house now, or are they renting one? Anyway, we should have a little capital to start with!! I always intended to save all my pay, but I never realised that I should be forced to do so! I wonder if you have found it possible to put anything by for the bottom draw? I fully realise that your living expenses have been high, but I am content in the knowledge that you have probably lived as well, if not better, than most people in England during these war years and that is what matters. My own mother died as a direct result of privations during 1914–18.

So, you were scared of the V1's! I should have been, too! When I think about the RAF's raids, I break out into a cold sweat – which is just about the same thing as your hot ones.

Silk stockings are definitely off – all over the world.

At Colombo they were not obtainable without Ceylon Govt. coupons and printed fabrics are also rationed. They were lisle, anyway, and cost 11/-pair.

At Suez they were unobtainable – and the bumboats brought more out at Port Said, which means there weren't any. There are no stockings in Thailand, except possibly American ones in Bangkok. Girls simply don't wear them. Ref, your legs – they will do whether they are covered or not – but preferably uncovered. Louise, I dare not put my thoughts down on paper. We have waited a long while and it seems incredible that soon I shall feel the glorious softness of your body close to mine again. I cannot tell you how many times I have relived our most intimate moments or the lasting happiness that you gave me in those never to be forgotten moments in August '41. I am terribly pleased that I didn't go abroad early in '41. Louie, you are very dear to me. And you are getting nearer, nearer, nearer every day.

Weekly 32 Off Portugal 6.X1.45
My Dearest,

A great glow in the night sky was all we saw of Lisbon last evening. Today, the weather has freshened, the wind has grown colder and the Atlantic is its typical self, with its great green walls of water following each other towards the distant cliffs of Portugal. The rollers aren't so large as the great green mountains, which tossed the Sobieski about off Newfoundland in 1941, but they are big enough. On the Sobieski, one could stand on the boat deck and be completely unable to see the rest *of the convoy except through the watery valleys. One's plate was put before one on the long table. Whoosh! About a dozen plates passed before one in quick succession. Whoosh! Back they came t'other way. It was rather like a cafeteria, except that the food moved and the recipient sat still . . . It isn't so bad yet, but, of course, we're not in the Bay of Biscay yet.*

We reach Liverpool late on Thursday night, but do not tie up at the landing stage until 2pm on Friday. I understand that the Orbita *will 'dress ship' as she comes up the Mersey and a reception of kinds awaits us. I am all for cutting out the nonsense and getting home. I believe we go the Huyton camps.*

I must phone you as soon as possible. What time shall we be free to phone? Will you have left the telephone address you have given me if it is late? Will there be telephones available in the Camp? When shall we leave for London? Will the 'processing' go on all night, leaving us free to travel on Saturday, or do we sleep on Friday night and go through the administrative processes during Saturday –making it Saturday night before we get away? When can you get away from Liverpool? I am determined to arrive after you at Shirley, because I have a great desire that you should be the one to open the door yourself. I understand from the Colonel, who has a Liverpool paper describing the arrival of the Tegelbourg, *that special trains to the various distributing centres start from Huyton itself and that we are not allowed into Liverpool.*

All these queries will be solved and answered within the next three days, so we won't worry about them. Au revoir, dear.

The *Orbita* picked up her pilot at Port Lynas, off Anglesey, and guided her up the River Mersey. The *Orbita* was dressed overall and all the way up the Mersey she was greeted with sounds of dozens of sirens and horns from the ships that lined the docks. At 2.30 p.m., the *Orbita* tied up and there to greet her at the dockside, were large crowds, cheering, shouting, laughing and crying.

In a quiet corner of a dockside shed, I found Louie.

Postscript

So Louise and Charles were reunited in a typically calm and quiet way. By coincidence, Captain Louise Steel and her company were stationed at Liverpool and had been involved in the details of the *Orbita*'s homecoming. After a brief parting, during which they rejoined their units, they were able to enjoy a lengthy leave together.

Finally demobbed in early 1946, Charles treasured the reference that Colonel Toosey gave him.

> *B.S.M. Charles W. Steel was under my command from 1ˢᵗ September 1941 until 19ᵗʰ November 1945.*
>
> *Before the Regiment went into action, he was a most valued and experienced NCO. During the battle of Malaya, he proved his worth conclusively. He did many responsible jobs excellently and with great courage.*
>
> *During the long period when we were POWs in Japanese hands, he carried out his duties in a most loyal and efficient manner. He never relaxed his high standard of behaviour for one moment under the most difficult conditions imaginable. I gave him most responsible jobs to do, which he invariably carried out in the most satisfactory way. He is a fine man, of sterling character. I cannot speak too highly of his character.*
>
> *Toosey, Lt-Col.R.A.*
> *Cmdg 135 Field Regiment R.A.*

Apart from attending the Victory Parade through London, this was about the last connection Charles had with the military. His application to wear the Territorial Army Long Service medal was refused, as he had missed out on its entitlement by a few months. Disappointed rather than surprised, he made a conscious effort to put his war experiences behind him and to focus on the future with Louise. He never joined a veterans' association nor participated in any reunions. Instead, he went about making up for lost time and rebuilding his life.

Louise's parents had died and their house had been left to her, which was a helpful start for the couple. Charles returned to the City and in May 1947 joined the stockbroking firm of L. Messel & Co., with whom he remained for the rest of his working life, eventually becoming a partner.

To their utter joy, Louise gave birth to a daughter, Margaret, in December 1948 and they felt their happiness to be complete. The family were living in Shirley, near Croydon, but later moved out to Tenterden in Kent, when Charles retired.

One of his objectives was to travel the world. In 1973, Charles and Louise visited Thailand. Charles wanted to travel the same route he had taken as a POW and to show his wife the places about which he had written so much. Learning of his visit, the Foreign Office arranged for the British Embassy in Bangkok to lay on a car and chauffeur. They were driven to Kanchanaburi, where they visited the large and beautifully maintained main POW Cemetery. They then went to Chungkai, Nong Pladuk, and, of course, Tamarkan.

Here they walked over the bridge, which had been repaired and strengthened after the war, ironically, by the Japanese. Sitting on the bank, with the bridge to their left, was the spot where the POWs were allowed their short yasme. The sun was just as fierce, the mountains just the same but a deep peace had replaced the noise and chaos of 1943.

Charles spoke of those terrible days without rancour but was deeply moved by his visit. He was also fascinated by one of the original locomotives used by the Japanese and the Road/Rail diesel lorries, with trucks, which were used during the railway's construction and were now a permanent exhibit.

They hired a motor riverboat and set off down the river to

Chungkai. Here they visited the cemetery and stood by the headstone of RSM Coles, whom Charles had helped bury. They later visited Nong Pladuk and found that the site of the camp was given over to a field of sugar cane.

They paid a second visit to Kanchanaburi, this time by train, which they caught at Nong Pladuk and travelled to the Bridge and, again, enjoyed the tranquility by the river. A final appointment in Bangkok saw Charles meeting Boon Pong and his daughter. In August 1945, Boon Pong's activities were exposed and he was arrested by the Japanese, imprisoned and sentenced to death. Fortunately, he was saved by the cessation of the war. When the Queen visited Thailand in 1972, she invited Boon Pong to dinner aboard the *Britannia*. For many years until he died, Boon Pong exchanged Christmas cards with Charles and his family.

In December 1975, Charles's former CO and hero, Philip Toosey, died in his sleep.

In 1979, the couple once again visited the Far East, this time Singapore and Malaysia. Charles showed Louise the places he had so graphically described in his letters. The YMCA Building, which had been the HQ of the Japanese Kempitai and the scene of much brutality. Another place to avoid in 1942 was Changi Post Office, which was used by the renegade Sikhs, who had lost no opportunity to impress upon the British POWs that there had been a change in status. At the rather neglected Singapore Railway Station, Charles stood on the very railway platform from where he and thousands of prisoners began their terrible three and a half-day journey to Ban Pong. Changi Prison still looked as grim and forbidding, while the nearby Roberts Barracks were peaceful in their quiet surroundings. They visited Bukit Timah and saw the reservoir, which is now within the exclusive Singapore Country Club. At the impressive Kranji War Cemetery, Charles paid his respects to those comrades of the 135th Field Regiment who were buried there. Leaving Singapore Island, they drove over the Causeway and into Malaysia and headed for Penang.

On the way, Charles stopped at the exact point where his

battery had fired from the edge of a rubber plantation across a field of pineapples at the advancing Japanese.

Now retired, Charles's interest in steam trains continued. In 1980, a journey on the Trans-Canada railway was something of a deciding moment for Charles for, on his return, he became a member and helper of the Kent and East Sussex Railway based at Tenterden. It was no surprise to the family when, at the age of seventy-three, he announced that he was taking an engine driver's course and went off to the Bluebell Railway, Sussex for a four day course. He arrived back home tired and happy – he was a qualified steam train driver.

Charles lived out the remainder of his life happily involved with the Railway and sharing Louise's interests in gardening, photography and local societies. He died in 1999 at the age of eighty-three and, amongst papers he kept in a safe, were his letters, which had only ever been read by Louise. Now we have shared that privilege and can only marvel at man's ability to rise above a seemingly vast ocean of despair and hopelessness and emerge with strength and dignity.

Bibliography

Goh Chor Boon, *Living Hell*, Asiapac Singapore 1999

John Coast, *Railway of Death*, Simpkin Marshall 1961

Peter N.Davies, *The Man Behind the Bridge – Colonel Toosey and the River Kwai,* Athlone Press 1991

Ernest Gordon, *Miracle on the River Kwai*, Collins 1963

Hardie, Dr Robert, *The Burma-Siam Railway – Secret Diary of Dr.Robert Hardie 1942–45*, Imperial War Museum 1983

Harries, Meiron and Susie, *Soldiers of the Sun – The Rise and Fall of the Imperial Japanese Army 1865–1945*, Heinemann 1991

Kinvig, Clifford, *River Kwai Railway – The Story of the Burma-Siam Railroad*, Brassey 1992

Lushington, Lieutenant Colonel Franklin, *Yeoman Service – A Short History of the Kent Yeomanry 1939–45*, The Medici Society 1947

Rivett, Rohan, *Behind Bamboo*, Angus & Robertson 1946

Stabolgi, Lord, RN, *Singapore and After* , Hutchinson 1942

Towle, Philip, Margaret Kosuge and Yoichi Kibata (eds.) *Japanese Prisoners of War*, Hambledon, 2000

Index